OXFORD

Series Editor: Victor Lee

William Wordsworth

William Wordsworth

Selected Poems

Edited by Sandra Anstey

Oxford University Press
1990

Oxford University Press, Walton Street, Oxford OX2 6DP

Oxford New York Toronto
Delhi Bombay Calcutta Madras Karachi
Kuala Lumpur Singapore Hong Kong Tokyo
Nairobi Dar es Salaam Cape Town
Melbourne Auckland

and associated companies in
Berlin Ibadan

Oxford is a trade mark of Oxford University Press

ISBN 0 19 8319517

The text for the poems is taken from
Wordsworth A Selection ed. Gill in the
Oxford Paperback series, by permission of the
Academic Division of O.U.P.

The publishers would like to thank the following
for permission to reproduce photographs:

Leicestershire Museums p. 173 (bottom);
The Mansell Collection p. 173 (top);
Pieterse-Davison International Ltd p. 170;
The Wordsworth Trust p. 171, 172.

The cover illustration is by Susan Scott.

Typeset by Pentacor PLC, High Wycombe, Bucks.
Printed in Great Britain by
M & A Thomson Litho Ltd., East Kilbride, Scotland.

Contents

Editors

Sandra Anstey taught English in one of the largest comprehensive schools in South Wales before her recent move to the post of Officer for English at the National Language Unit of Wales. After completing her doctoral thesis on R. S. Thomas, she edited a publication of critical writings about R. S. Thomas as well as an edition of his selected prose. She is Reviews Editor of *Poetry Wales*.

Dr Victor Lee, the Series Editor, read English at University College, Cardiff. He was awarded a doctorate at Oxford University. He has experience of teaching at Secondary and Tertiary level, and is currently working at the Open University. Victor Lee has been Chief Examiner in English for three examination boards over a period of twenty years.

Acknowledgements

I would like to thank Victor Lee, of the Open University, for his continued support and advice in the preparation of this book. I would also like to thank my pupils and colleagues.

Sandra Anstey

Foreword

Oxford Student Texts are specifically aimed at presenting poetry and drama to an audience which is studying English Literature at an advanced level. Each text is designed as an integrated whole consisting of three parts. The poetry or the play, always chronologically listed not thematically grouped, is always placed first to stress its importance and to encourage students to enjoy it without secondary critical material of any kind. When help is needed on other occasions, the second and third parts of these texts, the Notes and the Approaches, provide it.

The Notes perform two functions. Firstly, they provide information and explain allusions. Secondly, and this is where they differ from most texts at this level, they often raise questions of central concern to the interpretation of the poem or the play being dealt with, particularly in the use of a general note placed at the beginning of the particular notes.

The third part, the Approaches section, deals with major issues of response to the particular section of poetry or drama, as opposed to the work of the writer as a whole. One of the major aims of this part of the text is to emphasize that there is no one right answer to interpretations, but a series of approaches. Readers are given guidance as to what counts as evidence, but, in the end, left to make up their mind as to which are the most suitable interpretations, or to add their own.

To help achieve this, the Approaches section contains a number of activity-discussion sequences, although it must be stressed that these are optional. Significant issues about the poetry or the play are raised in these activities. The reader is invited to tackle these activities before proceeding to the discussion section where possible responses to the questions raised in the activities are considered. Their main function is to engage the reader actively in the ideas of the text. However, these activity-discussion sequences are so arranged that, if the readers wish to treat the Approaches as continuous prose and not attempt the activities, they can.

At the end of each text there is also a list of tasks. Whereas the activity-discussion sequences are aimed at increasing understanding of the literary work itself, these tasks are intended to help explore ideas about the poetry or the play after the student has completed the reading of the poems and the studying of the Notes and Approaches. These tasks are particularly helpful for coursework projects or in preparing for an examination.

Victor Lee   Series Editor

Poems

A Night-Piece

The sky is overspread
With a close veil of one continuous cloud
All whitened by the moon, that just appears,
A dim-seen orb, yet chequers not the ground
With any shadow—plant, or tower, or tree.
At last a pleasant instantaneous light
Startles the musing man whose eyes are bent
To earth. He looks around, the clouds are split
Asunder, and above his head he views
10   The clear moon and the glory of the heavens.
There in a black-blue vault she sails along
Followed by multitudes of stars, that small,
And bright, and sharp along the gloomy vault
Drive as she drives. How fast they wheel away!
Yet vanish not! The wind is in the trees;
But they are silent. Still they roll along
Immeasurably distant, and the vault
Built round by those white clouds, enormous clouds,
Still deepens its interminable depth.
20   At length the vision closes, and the mind
Not undisturbed by the deep joy it feels,
Which slowly settles into peaceful calm,
Is left to muse upon the solemn scene.

Lines

WRITTEN AT A SMALL DISTANCE FROM
MY HOUSE, AND SENT BY MY LITTLE BOY
TO THE PERSON TO WHOM THEY ARE
ADDRESSED

It is the first mild day of March:
Each minute sweeter than before,
The red-breast sings from the tall larch
That stands beside our door.

There is a blessing in the air,
Which seems a sense of joy to yield
To the bare trees, and mountains bare,
And grass in the green field.

My Sister! ('tis a wish of mine)
10 Now that our morning meal is done,
Make haste, your morning task resign;
Come forth and feel the sun.

Edward will come with you, and pray,
Put on with speed your woodland dress,
And bring no book, for this one day
We'll give to idleness.

No joyless forms shall regulate
Our living Calendar:
We from to-day, my friend, will date
20 The opening of the year.

Love, now an universal birth,
From heart to heart is stealing,
From earth to man, from man to earth,
—It is the hour of feeling.

One moment now may give us more
Than fifty years of reason;
Our minds shall drink at every pore
The spirit of the season.

Some silent laws our hearts may make,
30 Which they shall long obey;
We for the year to come may take
Our temper from to-day.

And from the blessed power that rolls
About, below, above;
We'll frame the measure of our souls,
They shall be tuned to love.

Then come, my sister! come, I pray,
With speed put on your woodland dress,
And bring no book; for this one day
40 We'll give to idleness.

Goody Blake and Harry Gill

A TRUE STORY

Oh! what's the matter? what's the matter?
What is't that ails young Harry Gill?
That evermore his teeth they chatter,
Chatter, chatter, chatter still.
Of waistcoats Harry has no lack,
Good duffle grey, and flannel fine;
He has a blanket on his back,
And coats enough to smother nine.

In March, December, and in July,
10   'Tis all the same with Harry Gill;
The neighbours tell, and tell you truly,
His teeth they chatter, chatter still,
At night, at morning, and at noon,
'Tis all the same with Harry Gill;
Beneath the sun, beneath the moon,
His teeth they chatter, chatter still.

Young Harry was a lusty drover,
And who so stout of limb as he?
His cheeks were red as ruddy clover,
20   His voice was like the voice of three.
Auld Goody Blake was old and poor,
Ill fed she was, and thinly clad;
And any man who passed her door,
Might see how poor a hut she had.

All day she spun in her poor dwelling,
And then her three hours' work at night!
Alas! 'twas hardly worth the telling,
It would not pay for candle-light.
—This woman dwelt in Dorsetshire,
30 Her hut was on a cold hill-side,
And in that country coals are dear,
For they come far by wind and tide.

By the same fire to boil their pottage,
Two poor old dames, as I have known,
Will often live in one small cottage,
But she, poor woman, dwelt alone.
'Twas well enough when summer came,
The long, warm, lightsome summer-day,
Then at her door the *canty* dame
40 Would sit, as any linnet gay.

But when the ice our streams did fetter,
Oh! then how her old bones would shake!
You would have said, if you had met her,
'Twas a hard time for Goody Blake.
Her evenings then were dull and dead;
Sad case it was, as you may think,
For very cold to go to bed,
And then for cold not sleep a wink.

Oh joy for her! when e'er in winter
50 The winds at night had made a rout,
And scattered many a lusty splinter,
And many a rotten bough about.
Yet never had she, well or sick,
As every man who knew her says,
A pile before-hand, wood or stick,
Enough to warm her for three days.

Now when the frost was past enduring,
And made her poor old bones to ache,
Could any thing be more alluring,
60   Than an old hedge to Goody Blake?
And now and then, it must be said,
When her old bones were cold and chill,
She left her fire, or left her bed,
To seek the hedge of Harry Gill.

Now Harry he had long suspected
This trespass of old Goody Blake,
And vowed that she should be detected,
And he on her would vengeance take.
And oft from his warm fire he'd go,
70   And to the fields his road would take,
And there, at night, in frost and snow,
He watched to seize old Goody Blake.

And once, behind a rick of barley,
Thus looking out did Harry stand;
The moon was full and shining clearly,
And crisp with frost the stubble-land.
—He hears a noise—he's all awake—
Again?—on tip-toe down the hill
He softly creeps—'Tis Goody Blake,
80   She's at the hedge of Harry Gill.
Right glad was he when he beheld her:
Stick after stick did Goody pull,
He stood behind a bush of elder,
Till she had filled her apron full.
When with her load she turned about,
The bye-road back again to take,
He started forward with a shout,
And sprang upon poor Goody Blake.

And fiercely by the arm he took her,
90 And by the arm he held her fast,
And fiercely by the arm he shook her,
And cried, 'I've caught you then at last!'
Then Goody, who had nothing said,
Her bundle from her lap let fall;
And kneeling on the sticks, she prayed
To God that is the judge of all.

She prayed, her withered hand uprearing,
While Harry held her by the arm—
'God! who art never out of hearing,
100 Oh may he never more be warm!'
The cold, cold moon above her head,
Thus on her knees did Goody pray,
Young Harry heard what she had said,
And icy-cold he turned away.

He went complaining all the morrow
That he was cold and very chill:
His face was gloom, his heart was sorrow,
Alas! that day for Harry Gill!
That day he wore a riding-coat,
110 But not a whit the warmer he:
Another was on Thursday brought,
And ere the Sabbath he had three.

'Twas all in vain, a useless matter,
And blankets were about him pinned;
Yet still his jaws and teeth they clatter,
Like a loose casement in the wind.
And Harry's flesh it fell away;
And all who see him say 'tis plain,
That, live as long as live he may,
120 He never will be warm again.

No word to any man he utters,
A-bed or up, to young or old;
But ever to himself he mutters,
'Poor Harry Gill is very cold.'
A-bed or up, by night or day;
His teeth they chatter, chatter still.
Now think, ye farmers all, I pray,
Of Goody Blake and Harry Gill.

'A whirl-blast from behind the hill'

A whirl-blast from behind the hill
Rushed o'er the wood with startling sound:
Then all at once the air was still,
And showers of hail-stones pattered round.
Where leafless Oaks towered high above,
I sate within an undergrove
Of tallest hollies, tall and green,
A fairer bower was never seen.
From year to year the spacious floor
10 With withered leaves is covered o'er,
You could not lay a hair between:
And all the year the bower is green.
But see! where'er the hailstones drop
The withered leaves all skip and hop,
There's not a breeze—no breath of air—
Yet here, and there, and every where
Along the floor, beneath the shade
By those embowering hollies made,
The leaves in myriads jump and spring,
20 As if with pipes and music rare
Some Robin Good-fellow were there,
And all those leaves, that jump and spring,
Were each a joyous, living thing.

Oh! grant me Heaven a heart at ease
That I may never cease to find,
Even in appearances like these
Enough to nourish and to stir my mind!

The Idiot Boy

'Tis eight o'clock, —a clear March night,
The moon is up—the sky is blue,
The owlet in the moonlight air,
He shouts from nobody knows where;
He lengthens out his lonely shout,
Halloo! halloo! a long halloo!

—Why bustle thus about your door,
What means this bustle, Betty Foy?
Why are you in this mighty fret?
10 And why on horseback have you set
Him whom you love, your idiot boy?

Beneath the moon that shines so bright,
Till she is tired, let Betty Foy
With girt and stirrup fiddle-faddle;
But wherefore set upon a saddle
Him whom she loves, her idiot boy?

There's scarce a soul that's out of bed;
Good Betty! put him down again;
His lips with joy they burr at you,
20 But Betty! what has he to do
With stirrup, saddle, or with rein?

The world will say 'tis very idle,
Bethink you of the time of night;
There's not a mother, no not one,
But when she hears what you have done,
Oh! Betty she'll be in a fright.

But Betty's bent on her intent,
For her good neighbour, Susan Gale,
Old Susan, she who dwells alone,
30   Is sick, and makes a piteous moan,
As if her very life would fail.

There's not a house within a mile,
No hand to help them in distress:
Old Susan lies a bed in pain,
And sorely puzzled are the twain,
For what she ails they cannot guess.

And Betty's husband's at the wood,
Where by the week he doth abide,
A woodman in the distant vale;
40   There's none to help poor Susan Gale,
What must be done? what will betide?

And Betty from the lane has fetched
Her pony, that is mild and good,
Whether he be in joy or pain,
Feeding at will along the lane,
Or bringing faggots from the wood.

And he is all in travelling trim,
And by the moonlight, Betty Foy
Has up upon the saddle set,
50   The like was never heard of yet,
Him whom she loves, her idiot boy.

And he must post without delay
Across the bridge that's in the dale.
And by the church, and o'er the down,
To bring a doctor from the town,
Or she will die, old Susan Gale.

There is no need of boot or spur,
There is no need of whip or wand,
For Johnny has his holly-bough,
60   And with a hurly-burly now
He shakes the green bough in his hand.

And Betty o'er and o'er has told
The boy who is her best delight,
Both what to follow, what to shun,
What do, and what to leave undone,
How turn to left, and how to right.

And Betty's most especial charge,
Was, 'Johnny! Johnny! mind that you
Come home again, nor stop at all,
70   Come home again, whate'er befal,
My Johnny do, I pray you do.'

To this did Johnny answer make,
Both with his head, and with his hand,
And proudly shook the bridle too,
And then! his words were not a few,
Which Betty well could understand.

And now that Johnny is just going,
Though Betty's in a mighty flurry,
She gently pats the pony's side,
80   On which her idiot boy must ride,
And seems no longer in a hurry.

But when the pony moves his legs,
Oh! then for the poor idiot boy!
For joy he cannot hold the bridle,
For joy his head and heels are idle,
He's idle all for very joy.

And while the pony moves his legs,
In Johnny's left-hand you may see,
The green bough's motionless and dead;
90   The moon that shines above his head
Is not more still and mute than he.

His heart it was so full of glee,
That till full fifty yards were gone,
He quite forgot his holly whip,
And all his skill in horsemanship,
Oh! happy, happy, happy, John.

And Betty's standing at the door,
And Betty's face with joy o'erflows,
Proud of herself, and proud of him,
100   She sees him in his travelling trim;
How quietly her Johnny goes.

The silence of her idiot boy,
What hopes it sends to Betty's heart!
He's at the guide-post—he turns right,
She watches till he's out of sight,
And Betty will not then depart.

Burr, burr—now Johnny's lips they burr,
As loud as any mill, or near it,
Meek as a lamb the pony moves,
110   And Johnny makes the noise he loves,
And Betty listens, glad to hear it.

Away she hies to Susan Gale:
And Johnny's in a merry tune,
The owlets hoot, the owlets curr,
And Johnny's lips they burr, burr, burr,
And on he goes beneath the moon.

His steed and he right well agree,
For of this pony there's a rumour,
That should he lose his eyes and ears,
120   And should he live a thousand years,
He never will be out of humour.

But then he is a horse that thinks!
And when he thinks his pace is slack;
Now, though he knows poor Johnny well,
Yet for his life he cannot tell
What he has got upon his back.

So through the moonlight lanes they go,
And far into the moonlight dale,
And by the church, and o'er the down,
130   To bring a doctor from the town,
To comfort poor old Susan Gale.

And Betty, now at Susan's side,
Is in the middle of her story,
What comfort Johnny soon will bring,
With many a most diverting thing,
Of Johnny's wit and Johnny's glory.

And Betty's still at Susan's side:
By this time she's not quite so flurried;
Demure with porringer and plate
140   She sits, as if in Susan's fate
Her life and soul were buried.

But Betty, poor good woman! she,
You plainly in her face may read it,
Could lend out of that moment's store
Five years of happiness or more,
To any that might need it.

But yet I guess that now and then
With Betty all was not so well,
And to the road she turns her ears,
150   And thence full many a sound she hears,
Which she to Susan will not tell.

Poor Susan moans, poor Susan groans,
'As sure as there's a moon in heaven,'
Cries Betty, 'he'll be back again;
They'll both be here, 'tis almost ten,
They'll both be here before eleven.'

Poor Susan moans, poor Susan groans,
The clock gives warning for eleven;
'Tis on the stroke—'If Johnny's near,'
160   Quoth Betty, 'he will soon be here,
As sure as there's a moon in heaven.'

The clock is on the stroke of twelve,
And Johnny is not yet in sight,
The moon's in heaven, as Betty sees,
But Betty is not quite at ease;
And Susan has a dreadful night.

And Betty, half an hour ago,
On Johnny vile reflections cast;
'A little idle sauntering thing!'
170   With other names, an endless string,
But now that time is gone and past.

And Betty's drooping at the heart,
That happy time all past and gone,
'How can it be he is so late?
The doctor he has made him wait,
Susan! they'll both be here anon.'

And Susan's growing worse and worse,
And Betty's in a sad quandary;
And then there's nobody to say
180   If she must go or she must stay:
—She's in a sad quandary.

The clock is on the stroke of one;
But neither Doctor nor his guide
Appear along the moonlight road,
There's neither horse nor man abroad,
And Betty's still at Susan's side.

And Susan she begins to fear
Of sad mischances not a few,
That Johnny may perhaps be drowned,
190   Or lost perhaps, and never found;
Which they must both for ever rue.

She prefaced half a hint of this
With 'God forbid it should be true!'
At the first word that Susan said
Cried Betty, rising from the bed,
'Susan, I'd gladly stay with you.

I must be gone, I must away,
Consider, Johnny's but half-wise;
Susan, we must take care of him,
200   If he is hurt in life or limb'—
'Oh God forbid!' poor Susan cries.

'What can I do?' says Betty, going,
'What can I do to ease your pain?
Good Susan tell me, and I'll stay;
I fear you're in a dreadful way,
But I shall soon be back again.'

'Good Betty go, good Betty go,
There's nothing that can ease my pain.'
Then off she hies, but with a prayer
210   That God poor Susan's life would spare,
Till she comes back again.

So, through the moonlight lane she goes,
And far into the moonlight dale;
And how she ran, and how she walked,
And all that to herself she talked,
Would surely be a tedious tale.

In high and low, above, below,
In great and small, in round and square,
In tree and tower was Johnny seen,
220   In bush and brake, in black and green,
'Twas Johnny, Johnny, every where.

She's past the bridge that's in the dale,
And now the thought torments her sore,
Johnny perhaps his horse forsook,
To hunt the moon that's in the brook,
And never will be heard of more.

And now she's high upon the down,
Alone amid a prospect wide;
There's neither Johnny nor his horse,
230   Among the fern or in the gorse;
There's neither doctor nor his guide.

'Oh saints! what is become of him?
Perhaps he's climbed into an oak,
Where he will stay till he is dead;
Or sadly he has been misled,
And joined the wandering gypsey-folk.

Or him that wicked pony's carried
To the dark cave, the goblins' hall,
Or in the castle he's pursuing,
240   Among the ghosts, his own undoing;
Or playing with the waterfall.'

At poor old Susan then she railed,
While to the town she posts away;
'If Susan had not been so ill,
Alas! I should have had him still,
My Johnny, till my dying day.'

Poor Betty! in this sad distemper,
The doctor's self would hardly spare,
Unworthy things she talked and wild,
250   Even he, of cattle of the most mild,
The pony had his share.

And now she's got into the town,
And to the doctor's door she hies;
'Tis silence all on every side;
The town so long, the town so wide,
Is silent as the skies.

And now she's at the doctor's door,
She lifts the knocker, rap, rap, rap,
The doctor at the casement shews,
260   His glimmering eyes that peep and doze;
And one hand rubs his old night-cap.

'Oh Doctor! Doctor! where's my Johnny?'
'I'm here, what is't you want with me?'
'Oh Sir! you know I'm Betty Foy,
And I have lost my poor dear boy,
You know him—him you often see;

He's not so wise as some folks be,'
'The devil take his wisdom!' said
The Doctor, looking somewhat grim,
270   'What, woman! should I know of him?'
And, grumbling, he went back to bed.

'O woe is me! O woe is me!
Here will I die; here will I die;
I thought to find my Johnny here,
But he is neither far nor near,
Oh! what a wretched mother I!'

She stops, she stands, she looks about,
Which way to turn she cannot tell.
Poor Betty! it would ease her pain
280   If she had heart to knock again;
—The clock strikes three—a dismal knell!

Then up along the town she hies,
No wonder if her senses fail,
This piteous news so much it shocked her,
She quite forgot to send the Doctor,
To comfort poor old Susan Gale.

And now she's high upon the down,
And she can see a mile of road,
'Oh cruel! I'm almost three-score;
290   Such night as this was ne'er before,
There's not a single soul abroad.'

She listens, but she cannot hear
The foot of horse, the voice of man;
The streams with softest sound are flowing,
The grass you almost hear it growing,
You hear it now if e'er you can.

The owlets through the long blue night
Are shouting to each other still:
Fond lovers, yet not quite hob nob,
300   They lengthen out the tremulous sob,
That echoes far from hill to hill.

Poor Betty now has lost all hope,
Her thoughts are bent on deadly sin;
A green-grown pond she just has passed,
And from the brink she hurries fast,
Lest she should drown herself therein.

And now she sits her down and weeps;
Such tears she never shed before;
'O dear, dear pony! my sweet joy!
310   Oh carry back my idiot boy!
And we will ne'er o'erload thee more.'

A thought is come into her head;
'The pony he is mild and good,
And we have always used him well;
Perhaps he's gone along the dell,
And carried Johnny to the wood.'

Then up she springs as if on wings;
She thinks no more of deadly sin;
If Betty fifty ponds should see,
320   The last of all her thoughts would be,
To drown herself therein.

Oh reader! now that I might tell
What Johnny and his horse are doing!
What they've been doing all this time,
Oh could I put it into rhyme,
A most delightful tale pursuing!

Perhaps, and no unlikely thought!
He with his pony now doth roam,
The cliffs and peaks so high that are,
330   To lay his hands upon a star,
And in his pocket bring it home.

Perhaps he's turned himself about,
His face unto his horse's tail,
And still and mute, in wonder lost,
All like a silent horseman-ghost,
He travels on along the vale.

And now, perhaps, he's hunting sheep,
A fierce and dreadful hunter he!
Yon valley, that's so trim and green,
340   In five months' time, should he be seen,
A desert wilderness will be.

Perhaps, with head and heels on fire,
And like the very sound of evil,
He's galloping away, away,
And so he'll gallop on for aye,
The bane of all that dread the devil.

I to the muses have been bound,
These fourteen years, by strong indentures;
Oh gentle muses! let me tell
350   But half of what to him befel,
For sure he met with strange adventures.

Oh gentle muses! is this kind?
Why will ye thus my suit repel?
Why of your further aid bereave me?
And can ye thus unfriended leave me?
Ye muses! whom I love so well.

Who's yon, that, near the waterfall,
Which thunders down with headlong force,
Beneath the moon, yet shining fair,
360 As careless as if nothing were,
Sits upright on a feeding horse?

Unto his horse, that's feeding free,
He seems, I think, the rein to give;
Of moon or stars he takes no heed;
Of such we in romances read,
—'Tis Johnny! Johnny! as I live.

And that's the very pony too.
Where is she, where is Betty Foy?
She hardly can sustain her fears;
370 The roaring water-fall she hears,
And cannot find her idiot boy.

Your pony's worth his weight in gold,
Then calm your terrors, Betty Foy!
She's coming from among the trees,
And now, all full in view, she sees
Him whom she loves, her idiot boy.

And Betty sees the pony too:
Why stand you thus Good Betty Foy?
It is not goblin, 'tis no ghost,
380 'Tis he whom you so long have lost,
He whom you love, your idiot boy.

She looks again—her arms are up—
She screams—she cannot move for joy;
She darts as with a torrent's force,
She almost has o'erturned the horse,
And fast she holds her idiot boy.

And Johnny burrs and laughs aloud,
Whether in cunning or in joy,
I cannot tell; but while he laughs,
390   Betty a drunken pleasure quaffs,
To hear again her idiot boy.

And now she's at the pony's tail,
And now she's at the pony's head,
On that side now, and now on this,
And almost stifled with her bliss,
A few sad tears does Betty shed.

She kisses o'er and o'er again,
Him whom she loves, her idiot boy,
She's happy here, she's happy there,
400   She's uneasy every where;
Her limbs are all alive with joy,

She pats the pony, where or when
She knows not, happy Betty Foy!
The little pony glad may be,
But he is milder far than she,
You hardly can perceive his joy,

'Oh! Johnny, never mind the Doctor,
You've done your best, and that is all.'
She took the reins, when this was said,
410   And gently turned the pony's head
From the loud water-fall.

By this the stars were almost gone,
The moon was setting on the hill,
So pale you scarcely looked at her:
The little birds began to stir,
Though yet their tongues were still.

The pony, Betty, and her boy,
Wind slowly through the woody dale:
And who is she, be-times abroad,
420   That hobbles up the steep rough road?
Who is it, but old Susan Gale?

Long Susan lay deep lost in thought,
And many dreadful fears beset her,
Both for her messenger and nurse;
And as her mind grew worse and worse,
Her body it grew better.

She turned, she tossed herself in bed,
On all sides doubts and terrors met her,
Point after point did she discuss;
430   And while her mind was fighting thus,
Her body still grew better.

'Alas! what is become of them?
These fears can never be endured,
I'll to the wood.'—The word scarce said,
Did Susan rise up from her bed,
As if by magic cured.

Away she posts up hill and down,
And to the wood at length is come,
She spies her friends, she shouts a greeting;
440   Oh me! it is a merry meeting,
As ever was in Christendom.

The owls have hardly sung their last,
While our four travellers homeward wend;
The owls have hooted all night long,
And with the owls began my song,
And with the owls must end.

For while they all were travelling home,
Cried Betty, 'Tell us Johnny do,
Where all this long night you have been,
450 What you have heard, what you have seen,
And Johnny, mind you tell us true.'

Now Johnny all night long had heard
The owls in tuneful concert strive;
No doubt too he the moon had seen;
For in the moonlight he had been
From eight o'clock till five.

And thus to Betty's question, he
Made answer, like a traveller bold,
(His very words I give to you,)
460 'The cocks did crow to-whoo, to-whoo,
And the sun did shine so cold.'
—Thus answered Johnny in his glory,
And that was all his travel's story.

Anecdote for Fathers

SHEWING HOW THE ART OF LYING MAY BE TAUGHT

I have a boy of five years old,
His face is fair and fresh to see;
His limbs are cast in beauty's mould,
And dearly he loves me.

One morn we strolled on our dry walk,
Our quiet house all full in view,
And held such intermitted talk
As we are wont to do.

My thoughts on former pleasures ran;
10   I thought of Kilve's delightful shore,
My pleasant home, when spring began,
A long, long year before.

A day it was when I could bear
To think, and think, and think again;
With so much happiness to spare,
I could not feel a pain.

My boy was by my side, so slim
And graceful in his rustic dress!
And oftentimes I talked to him,
20   In very idleness.

The young lambs ran a pretty race;
The morning sun shone bright and warm;
'Kilve', said I, 'was a pleasant place,
And so is Liswyn farm.

My little boy, which like you more,'
I said and took him by the arm—
'Our home by Kilve's delightful shore,
Or here at Liswyn farm?'

'And tell me, had you rather be,'
30   I said and held him by the arm,
'At Kilve's smooth shore by the green sea,
Or here at Liswyn farm?'

In careless mood he looked at me,
While still I held him by the arm,
And said, 'At Kilve I'd rather be
Than here at Liswyn farm.'

'Now, little Edward, say why so;
My little Edward, tell me why.'
'I cannot tell, I do not know.'
40   'Why this is strange,' said I.

'For, here are woods and green-hills warm;
There surely must some reason be
Why you would change sweet Liswyn farm
For Kilve by the green sea.'

At this, my boy, so fair and slim,
Hung down his head, nor made reply;
And five times did I say to him,
'Why? Edward, tell me why?'

His head he raised—there was in sight,
50   It caught his eye, he saw it plain—
Upon the house-top, glittering bright,
A broad and gilded vane.

Then did the boy his tongue unlock,
And thus to me he made reply;
'At Kilve there was no weather-cock,
And that's the reason why.'

O dearest, dearest boy! my heart
For better lore would seldom yearn,
Could I but teach the hundredth part
60 Of what from thee I learn.

We Are Seven

A simple child, dear brother Jim,
That lightly draws its breath,
And feels its life in every limb,
What should it know of death?

I met a little cottage girl,
She was eight years old, she said;
Her hair was thick with many a curl
That clustered round her head.

She had a rustic, woodland air,
10 And she was wildly clad;
Her eyes were fair, and very fair,
—Her beauty made me glad.

'Sisters and brothers, little maid,
How many may you be?'
'How many? seven in all,' she said,
And wondering looked at me.

'And where are they, I pray you tell?'
She answered, 'Seven are we,
And two of us at Conway dwell,
20   And two are gone to sea.

Two of us in the the church-yard lie,
My sister and my brother,
And in the church-yard cottage, I
Dwell near them with my mother.'

'You say that two at Conway dwell,
And two are gone to sea,
Yet you are seven; I pray you tell
Sweet Maid, how this may be?'

Then did the little Maid reply,
30   'Seven boys and girls are we;
Two of us in the church-yard lie,
Beneath the church-yard tree.'

'You run about, my little maid,
Your limbs they are alive;
If two are in the church-yard laid,
Then ye are only five.'

'Their graves are green, they may be seen,'
The little Maid replied,
'Twelve steps or more from my mother's door,
40   And they are side by side.

My stockings there I often knit,
My 'kerchief there I hem;
And there upon the ground I sit—
I sit and sing to them.

And often after sunset, Sir,
When it is light and fair,
I take my little porringer,
And eat my supper there.

The first that died was little Jane;
50   In bed she moaning lay,
Till God released her of her pain,
And then she went away.

So in the church-yard she was laid,
And all the summer dry,
Together round her grave we played,
My brother John and I.

And when the ground was white with snow,
And I could run and slide,
My brother John was forced to go,
60   And he lies by her side.'

'How many are you then,' said I,
'If they two are in Heaven?'
The little Maiden did reply,
'O Master! we are seven.'

'But they are dead; those two are dead!
Their spirits are in heaven!'
'Twas throwing words away; for still
The little Maid would have her will,
And said, 'Nay, we are seven!'

Expostulation and Reply

'Why William, on that old grey stone,
Thus for the length of half a day,
Why William, sit you thus alone,
And dream your time away?

Where are your books? that light bequeathed
To beings else forlorn and blind!
Up! Up! and drink the spirit breathed
From dead men to their kind.

You look round on your mother earth,
10 As if she for no purpose bore you;
As if you were her first-born birth,
And none had lived before you!'

One morning thus, by Esthwaite lake,
When life was sweet I knew not why,
To me my good friend Matthew spake,
And thus I made reply.

'The eye it cannot chuse but see,
We cannot bid the ear be still;
Our bodies feel, where'er they be,
20 Against, or with our will.

Nor less I deem that there are powers,
Which of themselves our minds impress,
That we can feed this mind of ours,
In a wise passiveness.

Think you, 'mid all this mighty sum
Of things for ever speaking,
That nothing of itself will come,
But we must still be seeking?

—Then ask not wherefore, here, alone,
30   Conversing as I may,
I sit upon this old grey stone,
And dream my time away.'

The Tables Turned

AN EVENING SCENE, ON THE SAME SUBJECT

Up! up! my friend, and clear your looks,
Why all this toil and trouble?
Up! up! my friend, and quit your books,
Or surely you'll grow double.

The sun above the mountain's head,
A freshening lustre mellow,
Through all the long green fields has spread,
His first sweet evening yellow.

Books! 'tis a dull and endless strife,
10   Come, hear the woodland linnet,
How sweet his music; on my life
There's more of wisdom in it.

And hark! how blithe the throstle sings!
And he is no mean preacher;
Come forth into the light of things,
Let Nature be your teacher.

She has a world of ready wealth,
Our minds and hearts to bless—
Spontaneous wisdom breathed by health,
20   Truth breathed by cheerfulness.

One impulse from a vernal wood
May teach you more of man;
Of moral evil and of good,
Than all the sages can.

Sweet is the lore which nature brings;
Our meddling intellect
Mis-shapes the beauteous forms of things;
—We murder to dissect.

Enough of science and of art;
30   Close up these barren leaves;
Come forth, and bring with you a heart
That watches and receives.

Lines written a few miles above Tintern Abbey

ON REVISITING THE BANKS OF THE WYE DURING A TOUR,
JULY 13, 1798

Five years have passed; five summers, with the length
Of five long winters! and again I hear
These waters, rolling from their mountain-springs
With a sweet inland murmur. —Once again
Do I behold these steep and lofty cliffs,
Which on a wild secluded scene impress
Thoughts of more deep seclusion; and connect
The landscape with the quiet of the sky.
The day is come when I again repose
10 Here, under this dark sycamore, and view
These plots of cottage-ground, these orchard-tufts,
Which, at this season, with their unripe fruits,
Among the woods and copses lose themselves,
Nor, with their green and simple hue, disturb
The wild green landscape. Once again I see
These hedge-rows, hardly hedge-rows, little lines
Of sportive wood run wild; these pastoral farms
Green to the very door; and wreathes of smoke
Sent up, in silence, from among the trees,
20 With some uncertain notice, as might seem,
Of vagrant dwellers in the houseless woods,
Or of some hermit's cave, where by this fire
The hermit sits alone.
                Though absent long,
These forms of beauty have not been to me,
As is a landscape to a blind man's eye:
But oft, in lonely rooms, and mid the din
Of towns and cities, I have owed to them,

In hours of weariness, sensations sweet,
Felt in the blood, and felt along the heart,
30   And passing even into my purer mind
With tranquil restoration:—feelings too
Of unremembered pleasure; such, perhaps,
As may have had no trivial influence
On that best portion of a good man's life;
His little, nameless, unremembered acts
Of kindness and of love. Nor less, I trust,
To them I may have owed another gift,
Of aspect more sublime; that blessed mood,
In which the burthen of the mystery,
40   In which the heavy and the weary weight
Of all this unintelligible world
Is lightened:—that serene and blessed mood,
In which the affections gently lead us on,
Until, the breath of this corporeal frame,
And even the motion of our human blood
Almost suspended, we are laid asleep
In body, and become a living soul:
While with an eye made quiet by the power
Of harmony, and the deep power of joy,
We see into the life of things.
50   If this
Be but a vain belief, yet, oh! how oft,
In darkness, and amid the many shapes
Of joyless day-light; when the fretful stir
Unprofitable, and the fever of the world,
Have hung upon the beatings of my heart,
How oft, in spirit, have I turned to thee

O sylvan Wye! Thou wanderer through the woods,
How often has my spirit turned to thee!
And now, with gleams of half-extinguished thought,

60   With many recognitions dim and faint,
     And somewhat of a sad perplexity,
     The picture of the mind revives again:
     While here I stand, not only with the sense
     Of present pleasure, but with pleasing thoughts
     That in this moment there is life and food
     For future years. And so I dare to hope
     Though changed, no doubt, from what I was, when first
     I came among these hills; when like a roe
     I bounded o'er the mountains, by the sides
70   Of the deep rivers, and the lonely streams,
     Wherever nature led; more like a man
     Flying from something that he dreads, than one
     Who sought the thing he loved. For nature then
     (The coarser pleasures of my boyish days,
     And their glad animal movements all gone by,)
     To me was all in all.—I cannot paint
     What then I was. The sounding cataract
     Haunted me like a passion: the tall rock,
     The mountain, and the deep and gloomy wood,
80   Their colours and their forms, were then to me
     An appetite: a feeling and a love,
     That had no need of a remoter charm,
     By thought supplied, or any interest
     Unborrowed from the eye.—That time is past,
     And all its aching joys are now no more,
     And all its dizzy raptures. Not for this
     Faint I, nor mourn nor murmur: other gifts
     Have followed, for such loss, I would believe,
     Abundant recompence. For I have learned
90   To look on nature, not as in the hour
     Of thoughtless youth, but hearing oftentimes
     The still, sad music of humanity,
     Not harsh nor grating, though of ample power

To chasten and subdue. And I have felt
A presence that disturbs me with the joy
Of elevated thoughts; a sense sublime
Of something far more deeply interfused,
Whose dwelling is the light of setting suns,
And the round ocean, and the living air,
100 And the blue sky, and in the mind of man,
A motion and a spirit, that impels
All thinking things, all objects of all thought,
And rolls through all things. Therefore am I still
A lover of the meadows and the woods,
And mountains; and of all that we behold
From this green earth; of all the mighty world
Of eye and ear, both what they half-create,
And what perceive; well pleased to recognize
In nature and the language of the sense,
110 The anchor of my purest thoughts, the nurse,
The guide, the guardian of my heart, and soul
Of all my moral being.

                Nor, perchance,
If I were not thus taught, should I the more
Suffer my genial spirits to decay:
For thou art with me, here, upon the banks
Of this fair river, thou, my dearest Friend,
My dear, dear Friend, and in thy voice I catch
The language of my former heart, and read
My former pleasures in the shooting lights
120 Of thy wild eyes. Oh! yet a little while
May I behold in thee what I was once,
My dear, dear Sister! And this prayer I make,
Knowing that Nature never did betray
The heart that loved her; 'tis her privilege,
Through all the years of this our life, to lead
From joy to joy: for she can so inform

The mind that is within us, so impress
With quietness and beauty, and so feed
With lofty thoughts, that neither evil tongues,
130   Rash judgments, nor the sneers of selfish men,
Nor greetings where no kindness is, nor all
The dreary intercourse of daily life,
Shall e'er prevail against us, or disturb
Our cheerful faith that all which we behold
Is full of blessings. Therefore let the moon
Shine on thee in thy solitary walk;
And let the misty mountain winds be free
To blow against thee: and in after years,
When these wild ecstasies shall be matured
140   Into a sober pleasure, when thy mind
Shall be a mansion for all lovely forms,
Thy memory be as a dwelling-place
For all sweet sounds and harmonies; Oh! then,
If solitude, or fear, or pain, or grief,
Should be thy portion, with what healing thoughts
Of tender joy wilt thou remember me,
And these my exhortations! Nor, perchance,
If I should be, where I no more can hear
Thy voice, nor catch from thy wild eyes these gleams
150   Of past existence, wilt thou then forget
That on the banks of this delightful stream
We stood together; and that I, so long
A worshipper of Nature, hither came,
Unwearied in that service: rather say
With warmer love, oh! with far deeper zeal
Of holier love. Nor wilt thou then forget,
That after many wanderings, many years
Of absence, these steep woods and lofty cliffs,
And this green pastoral landscape, were to me
160   More dear, both for themselves, and for thy sake.

'A slumber did my spirit seal'

A slumber did my spirit seal;
    I had no human fears;
She seemed a thing that could not feel
    The touch of earthly years.

No motion has she now, no force;
    She neither hears nor sees,
Rolled round in earth's diurnal course
    With rocks and stones and trees.

Song

She dwelt among th' untrodden ways
    Beside the springs of Dove,
A Maid whom there were none to praise
    And very few to love.

A Violet by a mossy stone
    Half-hidden from the Eye!
—Fair, as a star when only one
    Is shining in the sky!

She *lived* unknown, and few could know
10   When Lucy ceased to be;
But she is in her Grave, and Oh!
    The difference to me.

'Strange fits of passion I have known'

Strange fits of passion I have known,
And I will dare to tell,
But in the lover's ear alone,
What once to me befel.

When she I loved, was strong and gay
And like a rose in June,
I to her cottage bent my way,
Beneath the evening moon.

Upon the moon I fixed my eye
10   All over the wide lea;
My horse trudged on, and we drew nigh
Those paths so dear to me.

And now we reached the orchard plot,
And, as we climbed the hill,
Towards the roof of Lucy's cot
The moon descended still.

In one of those sweet dreams I slept,
Kind Nature's gentlest boon!
And, all the while, my eyes I kept
20   On the descending moon.

My horse moved on; hoof after hoof
He raised and never stopped:
When down behind the cottage roof
At once the planet dropped.

What fond and wayward thoughts will slide
Into a Lover's head—
'O mercy!' to myself I cried,
'If Lucy should be dead!'

Lucy Gray

Oft had I heard of Lucy Gray,
And when I crossed the Wild,
I chanced to see at break of day
The solitary Child.

No Mate, no comrade Lucy knew;
She dwelt on a wide Moor,
The sweetest Thing that ever grew
Beside a human door!

You yet may spy the Fawn at play,
10   The Hare upon the Green;
But the sweet face of Lucy Gray
Will never more be seen.

'To-night will be a stormy night,
You to the Town must go,
And take a lantern, Child, to light
Your Mother thro' the snow.'

'That, Father! will I gladly do;
'Tis scarcely afternoon—
The Minster-clock has just struck two,
20   And yonder is the Moon.'

At this the Father raised his hook
And snapped a faggot-band;
He plied his work, and Lucy took
The lantern in her hand.

Not blither is the mountain roe,
With many a wanton stroke
Her feet disperse the powd'ry snow
That rises up like smoke.

The storm came on before its time,
30   She wandered up and down,
And many a hill did Lucy climb
But never reached the Town.

The wretched Parents all that night
Went shouting far and wide;
But there was neither sound nor sight
To serve them for a guide.

At day-break on a hill they stood
That overlooked the Moor;
And thence they saw the Bridge of Wood
40   A furlong from their door.

And now they homeward turned, and cried
'In Heaven we all shall meet!'
When in the snow the Mother spied
The print of Lucy's feet.

Then downward from the steep hill's edge
They tracked the footmarks small;
And through the broken hawthorn-hedge,
And by the long stone-wall;

And then an open field they crossed,
50   The marks were still the same;
They tracked them on, nor ever lost,
And to the Bridge they came.

They followed from the snowy bank
The footmarks, one by one,
Into the middle of the plank,
And further there were none.

Yet some maintain that to this day
She is a living Child,
That you may see sweet Lucy Gray
60 Upon the lonesome Wild.

O'er rough and smooth she trips along,
And never looks behind;
And sings a solitary song
That whistles in the wind.

Nutting

——————————It seems a day,
One of those heavenly days which cannot die,
When forth I sallied from our cottage-door,
And with a wallet o'er my shoulder slung,
A nutting crook in hand, I turned my steps
Towards the distant woods, a Figure quaint,
Tricked out in proud disguise of Beggar's weeds
Put on for the occasion, by advice
And exhortation of my frugal Dame.
10 Motley accoutrements! of power to smile
At thorns, and brakes, and brambles, and, in truth,
More ragged than need was. Among the woods,
And o'er the pathless rocks, I forced my way
Until, at length, I came to one dear nook
Unvisited, where not a broken bough

Drooped with its withered leaves, ungracious sign
Of devastation, but the hazels rose
Tall and erect, with milk-white clusters hung,
A virgin scene!—A little while I stood,
20   Breathing with such suppression of the heart
As joy delights in; and with wise restraint
Voluptuous, fearless of a rival, eyed
The banquet, or beneath the trees I sate
Among the flowers, and with the flowers I played;
A temper known to those, who, after long
And weary expectation, have been blessed
With sudden happiness beyond all hope.—
—Perhaps it was a bower beneath whose leaves
The violets of five seasons re-appear
30   And fade, unseen by any human eye,
Where fairy water-breaks do murmur on
For ever, and I saw the sparkling foam,
And with my cheek on one of those green stones
That, fleeced with moss, beneath the shady trees,
Lay round me scattered like a flock of sheep,
I heard the murmur and the murmuring sound,
In that sweet mood when pleasure loves to pay
Tribute to ease, and, of its joy secure
The heart luxuriates with indifferent things,
40   Wasting its kindliness on stocks and stones,
And on the vacant air. Then up I rose,
And dragged to earth both branch and bough,
   with crash
And merciless ravage; and the shady nook
Of hazels, and the green and mossy bower,
Deformed and sullied, patiently gave up
Their quiet being: and unless I now
Confound my present feelings with the past,
Even then, when from the bower I turned away,

Exulting, rich beyond the wealth of kings
50 I felt a sense of pain when I beheld
The silent trees and the intruding sky. —

    Then, dearest Maiden! move along these shades
In gentleness of heart; with gentle hand
Touch, ——for there is a Spirit in the woods.

'Three years she grew in sun and shower'

Three years she grew in sun and shower,
Then Nature said, 'A lovelier flower
On earth was never sown;
This Child I to myself will take,
She shall be mine, and I will make
A Lady of my own.

Myself will to my darling be
Both law and impulse, and with me
The Girl in rock and plain,
10 In earth and heaven, in glade and bower,
Shall feel an overseeing power
To kindle or restrain.

She shall be sportive as the fawn
That wild with glee across the lawn
Or up the mountain springs,
And hers shall be the breathing balm,
And hers the silence and the calm
Of mute insensate things.

The floating clouds their state shall lend
20 To her, for her the willow bend,
Nor shall she fail to see
Even in the motions of the storm
A beauty that shall mould her form
By silent sympathy.

The stars of midnight shall be dear
To her, and she shall lean her ear
In many a secret place
Where rivulets dance their wayward round,
And beauty born of murmuring sound
30 Shall pass into her face.

And vital feelings of delight
Shall rear her form to stately height,
Her virgin bosom swell,
Such thoughts to Lucy I will give
While she and I together live
Here in this happy dell.'

Thus Nature spake—The work was done—
How soon my Lucy's race was run!
She died and left to me
40 This heath, this calm and quiet scene,
The memory of what has been,
And never more will be.

Rural Architecture

There's George Fisher, Charles Fleming, and Reginald
    Shore,
Three rosy-cheeked School-boys, the highest not more
Than the height of a Counsellor's bag;
To the top of Great How did it please them to climb,
And there they built up without mortar or lime
A Man on the peak of the crag.

They built him of stones gathered up as they lay,
They built him and christened him all in one day,
An Urchin both vigorous and hale;
10 And so without scruple they called him Ralph Jones.
Now Ralph is renowned for the length of his bones;
The Magog of Legberthwaite dale.

Just half a week after the Wind sallied forth,
And, in anger or merriment, out of the North
Coming on with a terrible pother,
From the peak of the crag blew the Giant away.
And what did these School-boys?—The very next day
They went and they built up another.

—Some little I've seen of blind boisterous works
20 In Paris and London, 'mong Christians or Turks,
Spirits busy to do and undo:
At remembrance whereof my blood sometimes will flag.
—Then, light-hearted Boys, to the top of the Crag!
And I'll build up a Giant with you.

Michael

A PASTORAL POEM

If from the public way you turn your steps
Up the tumultuous brook of Green-head Gill,
You will suppose that with an upright path
Your feet must struggle; in such bold ascent
The pastoral Mountains front you, face to face.
But, courage! for beside that boisterous Brook
The mountains have all opened out themselves,
And made a hidden valley of their own.
No habitation there is seen; but such
10   As journey thither find themselves alone
With a few sheep, with rocks and stones, and kites
That overhead are sailing in the sky.
It is in truth an utter solitude,
Nor should I have made mention of this Dell
But for one object which you might pass by,
Might see and notice not. Beside the brook
There is a straggling heap of unhewn stones!
And to that place a story appertains,
Which, though it be ungarnished with events,
20   Is not unfit, I deem, for the fire-side,
Or for the summer shade. It was the first,
The earliest of those tales that spake to me
Of Shepherds, dwellers in the vallies, men
Whom I already loved, not verily
For their own sakes, but for the fields and hills
Where was their occupation and abode.
And hence this Tale, while I was yet a boy
Careless of books, yet having felt the power
Of Nature, by the gentle agency

30   Of natural objects led me on to feel
      For passions that were not my own, and think
      At random and imperfectly indeed
      On man; the heart of man and human life.
      Therefore, although it be a history
      Homely and rude, I will relate the same
      For the delight of a few natural hearts,
      And with yet fonder feeling, for the sake
      Of youthful Poets, who among these Hills
      Will be my second self when I am gone.

40   Upon the Forest-side in Grasmere Vale
      There dwelt a Shepherd, Michael was his name,
      An old man, stout of heart, and strong of limb.
      His bodily frame had been from youth to age
      Of an unusual strength: his mind was keen
      Intense and frugal, apt for all affairs,
      And in his Shepherd's calling he was prompt
      And watchful more than ordinary men.
      Hence he had learned the meaning of all winds,
      Of blasts of every tone, and often-times
50   When others heeded not, he heard the South
      Make subterraneous music, like the noise
      Of Bagpipers on distant Highland hills;
      The Shepherd, at such warning, of his flock
      Bethought him, and he to himself would say
      The winds are now devising work for me!
      And truly at all times the storm, that drives
      The Traveller to a shelter, summoned him
      Up to the mountains: he had been alone
      Amid the heart of many thousand mists
60   That came to him and left him on the heights.
      So lived he till his eightieth year was passed.

And grossly that man errs, who should suppose
That the green Valleys, and the Streams and Rocks
Were things indifferent to the Shepherd's thoughts.
Fields, where with cheerful spirits he had breathed
The common air; the hills, which he so oft
Had climbed with vigorous steps; which had impressed
So many incidents upon his mind
Of hardship, skill or courage, joy or fear;
70   Which like a book preserved the memory
Of the dumb animals, whom he had saved,
Had fed or sheltered, linking to such acts,
So grateful in themselves, the certainty
Of honorable gains; these fields, these hills
Which were his living Being, even more
Than his own Blood—what could they less? had laid
Strong hold on his affections, were to him
A pleasurable feeling of blind love,
The pleasure which there is in life itself.

80   He had not passed his days in singleness.
He had a Wife, a comely Matron, old
Though younger than himself full twenty years.
She was a woman of a stirring life
Whose heart was in her house: two wheels she had
Of antique form, this large for spinning wool,
That small for flax, and if one wheel had rest,
It was because the other was at work.
The Pair had but one Inmate in their house,
An only Child, who had been born to them
90   When Michael telling o'er his years began
To deem that he was old, in Shepherd's phrase,
With one foot in the grave. This only son,
With two brave sheep dogs tried in many a storm,
The one of an inestimable worth,
Made all their Household. I may truly say,

That they were as a proverb in the vale
For endless industry. When day was gone,
And from their occupations out of doors
The Son and Father were come home, even then
100   Their labour did not cease, unless when all
Turned to their cleanly supper-board, and there
Each with a mess of pottage and skimmed milk,
Sate round their basket piled with oaten cakes,
And their plain home-made cheese. Yet when their meal
Was ended, Luke (for so the Son was named)
And his old Father, both betook themselves
To such convenient work, as might employ
Their hands by the fire-side; perhaps to card
Wool for the House-wife's spindle, or repair
110   Some injury done to sickle, flail, or scythe,
Or other implement of house or field.

Down from the ceiling by the chimney's edge,
Which in our ancient uncouth country style
Did with a huge projection overbrow
Large space beneath, as duly as the light
Of day grew dim, the House-wife hung a lamp;
An aged utensil, which had performed
Service beyond all others of its kind.
Early at evening did it burn and late,
120   Surviving Comrade of uncounted Hours
Which going by from year to year had found
And left the Couple neither gay perhaps
Nor chearful, yet with objects and with hopes
Living a life of eager industry.
And now, when Luke was in his eighteenth year,
There by the light of this old lamp they sate,
Father and Son, while late into the night
The House-wife plied her own peculiar work,
Making the cottage thro' the silent hours

130   Murmur as with the sound of summer flies.
Not with a waste of words, but for the sake
Of pleasure, which I know that I shall give
To many living now, I of this Lamp
Speak thus minutely: for there are no few
Whose memories will bear witness to my tale.
The Light was famous in its neighbourhood,
And was a public Symbol of the life,
The thrifty Pair had lived. For, as it chanced,
Their Cottage on a plot of rising ground
140   Stood single, with large prospect North and South,
High into Easedale, up to Dunmal-Raise,
And Westward to the village near the Lake.
And from this constant light so regular
And so far seen, the House itself by all
Who dwelt within the limits of the vale,
Both old and young, was named the Evening Star.

Thus living on through such a length of years,
The Shepherd, if he loved himself, must needs
Have loved his Help-mate; but to Michael's heart
150   This Son of his old age was yet more dear—
Effect which might perhaps have been produced
By that instinctive tenderness, the same
Blind Spirit, which is in the blood of all,
Or that a child, more than all other gifts,
Brings hope with it, and forward-looking thoughts,
And stirrings of inquietude, when they
By tendency of nature needs must fail.
From such, and other causes, to the thoughts
Of the old Man his only Son was now
160   The dearest object that he knew on earth.
Exceeding was the love he bare to him,
His Heart and his Heart's joy! For oftentimes
Old Michael, while he was a babe in arms,

Had done him female service, not alone
For dalliance and delight, as is the use
Of Fathers, but with patient mind enforced
To acts of tenderness; and he had rocked
His cradle with a woman's gentle hand.

And in a later time, ere yet the Boy
170   Had put on Boy's attire, did Michael love,
Albeit of a stern unbending mind,
To have the young one in his sight, when he
Had work by his own door, or when he sate
With sheep before him on his Shepherd's stool,
Beneath that large old Oak, which near their door
Stood, and from its enormous breadth of shade
Chosen for the Shearer's covert from the sun,
Thence in our rustic dialect was called
The CLIPPING TREE, a name which yet it bears.
180   There, while they two were sitting in the shade,
With others round them, earnest all and blithe,
Would Michael exercise his heart with looks
Of fond correction and reproof bestowed
Upon the child, if he disturbed the sheep
By catching at their legs, or with his shouts
Scared them, while they lay still beneath the shears.

And when by Heaven's good grace the Boy grew up
A healthy Lad, and carried in his cheek
Two steady roses that were five years old,
190   Then Michael from a winter coppice cut
With his own hand a sapling, which he hooped
With iron, making it throughout in all
Due requisites a perfect Shepherd's Staff,
And gave it to the Boy; wherewith equipped
He as a Watchman oftentimes was placed
At gate or gap, to stem or turn the flock,

And to his office prematurely called
There stood the urchin, as you will divine,
Something between a hindrance and a help,
200 And for this cause not always, I believe,
Receiving from his Father hire of praise.
Though nought was left undone, which staff or voice,
Or looks, or threatening gestures could perform.
    But soon as Luke, full ten years old, could stand
Against the mountain blasts, and to the heights,
Not fearing toil, nor length of weary ways,
He with his Father daily went, and they
Were as companions, why should I relate
That objects which the Shepherd loved before
210 Were dearer now? that from the Boy there came
Feelings and emanations, things which were
Light to the sun and music to the wind;
And that the Old Man's heart seemed born again.
    Thus in his Father's sight the Boy grew up:
And now when he had reached his eighteenth year,
He was his comfort and his daily hope.

While this good household thus were living on
From day to day, to Michael's ear there came
Distressful tidings. Long before the time
220 Of which I speak, the Shepherd had been bound
In surety for his Brother's Son, a man
Of an industrious life, and ample means,
But unforeseen misfortunes suddenly
Had pressed upon him, and old Michael now
Was summoned to discharge the forfeiture,
A grievous penalty, but little less
Than half his substance. This un-looked for claim
At the first hearing, for a moment took
More hope out of his life than he supposed

230   That any old man ever could have lost.
     As soon as he had gathered so much strength
     That he could look his trouble in the face,
     It seemed that his sole refuge was to sell
     A portion of his patrimonial fields.
     Such was his first resolve; he thought again,
     And his heart failed him. 'Isabel,' said he,
     Two evenings after he had heard the news,
     'I have been toiling more than seventy years,
     And in the open sun-shine of God's love
240   Have we all lived, yet if these fields of ours
     Should pass into a Stranger's hand, I think
     That I could not lie quiet in my grave.
     Our lot is a hard lot; the Sun itself
     Has scarcely been more diligent than I,
     And I have lived to be a fool at last
     To my own family. An evil Man
     That was, and made an evil choice, if he
     Were false to us; and if he were not false,
     There are ten thousand to whom loss like this
250   Had been no sorrow. I forgive him—but
     'Twere better to be dumb than to talk thus.
     When I began, my purpose was to speak
     Of remedies and of a chearful hope.
     Our Luke shall leave us, Isabel; the land
     Shall not go from us, and it shall be free,
     He shall possess it, free as is the wind
     That passes over it. We have, thou knowest,
     Another Kinsman, he will be our friend
     In this distress. He is a prosperous man,
260   Thriving in trade, and Luke to him shall go,
     And with his Kinsman's help and his own thrift,
     He quickly will repair this loss, and then
     May come again to us. If here he stay,

What can be done? Where every one is poor
What can be gained?' At this, the old man paused,
And Isabel sate silent, for her mind
Was busy, looking back into past times.
There's Richard Bateman, thought she to herself,
He was a parish-boy—at the church-door
270 They made a gathering for him, shillings, pence,
And halfpennies, wherewith the Neighbours bought
A Basket, which they filled with Pedlar's wares,
And with this Basket on his arm, the Lad
Went up to London, found a Master there,
Who out of many chose the trusty Boy
To go and overlook his merchandise
Beyond the seas, where he grew wond'rous rich,
And left estates and monies to the poor,
And at his birth-place built a Chapel, floored
280 With Marble, which he sent from foreign lands.
These thoughts, and many others of like sort,
Passed quickly thro' the mind of Isabel,
And her face brightened. The Old Man was glad,
And thus resumed. 'Well! Isabel, this scheme
These two days has been meat and drink to me.
Far more than we have lost is left us yet.
—We have enough—I wish indeed that I
Were younger, but this hope is a good hope.
—Make ready Luke's best garments, of the best
290 Buy for him more, and let us send him forth
To-morrow, or the next day, or to-night:
—If he could go, the Boy should go to-night.'
Here Michael ceased, and to the fields went forth
With a light heart. The House-wife for five days
Was restless morn and night, and all day long
Wrought on with her best fingers to prepare

Things needful for the journey of her Son.
But Isabel was glad when Sunday came
To stop her in her work; for, when she lay
300 By Michael's side, she for the two last nights
Heard him, how he was troubled in his sleep:
And when they rose at morning she could see
That all his hopes were gone. That day at noon
She said to Luke, while they two by themselves
Were sitting at the door, 'Thou must not go,
We have no other Child but thee to lose,
None to remember—do not go away,
For if thou leave thy Father he will die.'
The Lad made answer with a jocund voice,
310 And Isabel, when she had told her fears,
Recovered heart. That evening her best fare
Did she bring forth, and all together sate
Like happy people round a Christmas fire.

Next morning Isabel resumed her work,
And all the ensuing week the house appeared
As cheerful as a grove in Spring: at length
The expected letter from their Kinsman came,
With kind assurances that he would do
His utmost for the welfare of the Boy,
320 To which requests were added that forthwith
He might be sent to him. Ten times or more
The letter was read over; Isabel
Went forth to shew it to the neighbours round:
Nor was there at that time on English Land
A prouder heart than Luke's. When Isabel
Had to her house returned, the Old Man said
'He shall depart to-morrow.' To this word
The House-wife answered, talking much of things

Which, if at such short notice he should go,
330   Would surely be forgotten. But at length
She gave consent, and Michael was at ease.
Near the tumultuous brook of Green-head Gill,
In that deep Valley, Michael had designed
To build a Sheep-fold, and, before he heard
The tidings of his melancholy loss,
For this same purpose he had gathered up
A heap of stones, which close to the brook side
Lay thrown together, ready for the work.
With Luke that evening thitherward he walked;
340   And soon as they had reached the placed he stopped
And thus the Old Man spake to him. 'My Son,
To-morrow thou wilt leave me; with full heart
I look upon thee, for thou art the same
That wert a promise to me ere thy birth,
And all thy life hast been my daily joy.
I will relate to thee some little part
Of our two histories; 'twill do thee good
When thou art from me, even if I should speak
Of things thou canst not know of. —After thou
350   First cam'st into the world, as it befalls
To new-born infants, thou didst sleep away
Two days, and blessings from thy Father's tongue
Then fell upon thee. Day by day passed on,
And still I loved thee with encreasing love.
Never to living ear came sweeter sounds
Than when I heard thee by our own fire-side
First uttering without words a natural tune,
When thou, a feeding babe, didst in thy joy
Sing at thy Mother's breast. Month followed month,
360   And in the open fields my life was passed
And in the mountains, else I think that thou

Hadst been brought up upon thy father's knees.
—But we were playmates, Luke; among these hills,
As well thou know'st, in us the old and young
Have played together, nor with me didst thou
Lack any pleasure which a boy can know.'
Luke had a manly heart, but at these words
He sobbed aloud; the Old Man grasped his hand,
And said, 'Nay do not take it so—I see
370 That these are things of which I need not speak.
—Even to the utmost I have been to thee
A kind and a good Father: and herein
I but repay a gift which I myself
Received by others hands, for, though now old
Beyond the common life of man, I still
Remember them who loved me in my youth.
Both of them sleep together: here they lived
As all their Forefathers had done, and when
At length their time was come, they were not loth
380 To give their bodies to the family mold.
I wished that thou should'st live the life they lived.
But 'tis a long time to look back, my Son,
And see so little gain from sixty years.
These fields were burthened when they came to me;
'Till I was forty years of age, not more
Than half of my inheritance was mine.
I toiled and toiled; God blessed me in my work,
And 'till these three weeks past the land was free.
—It looks as if it never could endure
390 Another Master, Heaven forgive me, Luke,
If I judge ill for thee, but it seems good
That thou should'st go.' At this the Old Man paused,
Then, pointing to the Stones near which they stood,
Thus, after a short silence, he resumed:

'This was a work for us, and now, my Son,
It is a work for me. But, lay one Stone—
Here, lay it for me, Luke, with thine own hands.
I for the purpose brought thee to this place.
Nay, Boy, be of good hope:—we both may live
400 To see a better day. At eighty-four
I still am strong and stout;—do thou thy part,
I will do mine.—I will begin again
With many tasks that were resigned to thee;
Up to the heights, and in among the storms,
Will I without thee go again, and do
All works which I was wont to do alone,
Before I knew thy face.—Heaven bless thee, Boy!
Thy heart these two weeks has been beating fast
With many hopes—it should be so—yes—yes—
410 I knew that thou could'st never have a wish
To leave me, Luke, thou hast been bound to me
Only by links of love, when thou art gone
What will be left to us!—But, I forget
My purposes. Lay now the corner-stone,
As I requested, and hereafter, Luke,
When thou art gone away, should evil men
Be thy companions, let this Sheep-fold be
Thy anchor and thy shield; amid all fear
And all temptation, let it be to thee
420 An emblem of the life thy Fathers lived,
Who, being innocent, did for that cause
Bestir them in good deeds. Now, fare thee well—
When thou return'st, thou in this place wilt see
A work which is not here, a covenant
'Twill be between us—but whatever fate
Befall thee, I shall love thee to the last,
And bear thy memory with me to the grave.'

The Shepherd ended here; and Luke stooped down,
And as his Father had requested, laid
430   The first stone of the Sheep-fold; at the sight
The Old Man's grief broke from him, to his heart
He pressed his Son, he kissed him and wept;
And to the House together they returned.

Next morning, as had been resolved, the Boy
Began his journey, and when he had reached
The public Way, he put on a bold face;
And all the Neighbours as he passed their doors
Came forth, with wishes and with farewell prayers,
That followed him 'till he was out of sight.
440   A good report did from their Kinsman come,
Of Luke and his well-doing; and the Boy
Wrote loving letters, full of wond'rous news,
Which, as the House-wife phrased it, were throughout
The prettiest letters that were ever seen.
Both parents read them with rejoicing hearts.
So, many months passed on: and once again
The Shepherd went about his daily work
With confident and cheerful thoughts; and now
Sometimes when he could find a leisure hour
450   He to that valley took his way, and there
Wrought at the Sheep-fold. Meantime Luke began
To slacken in his duty, and at length
He in the dissolute city gave himself
To evil courses: ignominy and shame
Fell on him, so that he was driven at last
To seek a hiding-place beyond the seas.

There is a comfort in the strength of love;
'Twill make a thing endurable, which else
Would break the heart:—Old Michael found it so.

460 I have conversed with more than one who well
     Remember the Old Man, and what he was
     Years after he had heard this heavy news.
     His bodily frame had been from youth to age
     Of an unusual strength. Among the rocks
     He went, and still looked up upon the sun,
     And listened to the wind; and as before
     Performed all kinds of labour for his Sheep,
     And for the land his small inheritance.
     And to that hollow Dell from time to time
470 Did he repair, to build the Fold of which
     His flock had need. 'Tis not forgotten yet
     The pity which was then in every heart
     For the Old Man—and 'tis believed by all
     That many and many a day he thither went,
     And never lifted up a single stone.
     There, by the Sheep-fold, sometimes was he seen
     Sitting alone, with that his faithful Dog,
     Then old, beside him, lying at his feet.
     The length of full seven years from time to time
480 He at the building of this Sheep-fold wrought,
     And left the work unfinished when he died.

     Three years, a little more, did Isabel,
     Survive her Husband: at her death the estate
     Was sold, and went into a Stranger's hand.
     The Cottage which was named The Evening Star
     Is gone, the ploughshare has been through the ground
     On which it stood; great changes have been wrought
     In all the neighbourhood, yet the Oak is left
     That grew beside their Door; and the remains
490 Of the unfinished Sheep-fold may be seen
     Beside the boisterous brook of Green-head Gill.

'I travelled among unknown Men'

I travelled among unknown Men,
    In Lands beyond the Sea;
Nor England! did I know till then
    What love I bore to thee.

'Tis past, that melancholy dream!
    Nor will I quit thy shore
A second time; for still I seem
    To love thee more and more.

Among thy mountains did I feel
10   The joy of my desire;
And She I cherished turned her wheel
    Beside an English fire.

Thy mornings shewed—thy nights concealed
    The bowers where Lucy played;
And thine is, too, the last green field
    Which Lucy's eyes surveyed!

'My heart leaps up when I behold'

My heart leaps up when I behold
    A Rainbow in the sky:
So was it when my life began;
So is it now I am a Man;
So be it when I shall grow old,
    Or let me die!
The Child is Father of the Man;
And I could wish my days to be
Bound each to each by natural piety.

Resolution and Independence

There was a roaring in the wind all night;
The rain came heavily and fell in floods;
But now the sun is rising calm and bright;
The birds are singing in the distant woods;
Over his own sweet voice the Stock-dove broods;
The Jay makes answer as the Magpie chatters;
And all the air is filled with pleasant noise of waters.

All things that love the sun are out of doors;
The sky rejoices in the morning's birth;
10   The grass is bright with rain-drops; on the moors
The Hare is running races in her mirth;
And with her feet she from the plashy earth
Raises a mist; which, glittering in the sun,
Runs with her all the way, wherever she doth run.

I was a Traveller then upon the moor;
I saw the Hare that raced about with joy;
I heard the woods, and distant waters, roar;
Or heard them not, as happy as a Boy:
The pleasant season did my heart employ:
20   My old remembrances went from me wholly;
And all the ways of men, so vain and melancholy.

But, as it sometimes chanceth, from the might
Of joy in minds that can no farther go,
As high as we have mounted in delight
In our dejection do we sink as low,
To me that morning did it happen so;
And fears, and fancies, thick upon me came;
Dim sadness, and blind thoughts I knew not nor could
    name.

I heard the Sky-lark singing in the sky;
30 And I bethought me of the playful Hare:
Even such a happy Child of earth am I;
Even as these blissful Creatures do I fare;
Far from the world I walk, and from all care;
But there may come another day to me,
Solitude, pain of heart, distress, and poverty.

My whole life I have lived in pleasant thought,
As if life's business were a summer mood;
As if all needful things would come unsought
To genial faith, still rich in genial good;
40 But how can He expect that others should
Build for him, sow for him, and at his call
Love him, who for himself will take no heed at all?

I thought of Chatterton, the marvellous Boy,
The sleepless Soul that perished in its pride;
Of Him who walked in glory and in joy
Behind his plough, upon the mountain-side;
By our own spirits are we deified;
We Poets in our youth begin in gladness;
But thereof comes in the end despondency and
    madness.

50 Now, whether it were by peculiar grace,
A leading from above, a something given,
Yet it befel, that, in this lonely place,
When up and down my fancy thus was driven,
And I with these untoward thoughts had striven,
I saw a Man before me unawares:
The oldest Man he seemed that ever wore grey hairs.

My course I stopped as soon as I espied
The Old Man in that naked wilderness:
Close by a Pond, upon the further side,
60 He stood alone: a minute's space I guess
I watched him, he continuing motionless:
To the Pool's further margin then I drew;
He being all the while before me full in view.

As a huge Stone is sometimes seen to lie
Couched on the bald top of an eminence;
Wonder to all who do the same espy
By what means it could thither come, and whence;
So that it seems a thing endued with sense:
Like a Sea-beast crawled forth, which on a shelf
70 Of rock or sand reposeth, there to sun itself.

Such seemed this Man, not all alive nor dead,
Nor all asleep; in his extreme old age:
His body was bent double, feet and head
Coming together in their pilgrimage;
As if some dire constraint of pain, or rage
Of sickness felt by him in times long past,
A more than human weight upon his frame had cast.

Himself he propped, his body, limbs, and face,
Upon a long grey Staff of shaven wood:
80 And, still as I drew near with gentle pace,
Beside the little pond or moorish flood
Motionless as a Cloud the Old Man stood;
That heareth not the loud winds when they call;
And moveth altogether, if it move at all.

At length, himself unsettling, he the Pond
Stirred with his Staff, and fixedly did look
Upon the muddy water, which he conned,
As if he had been reading in a book:
And now such freedom as I could I took;
90 And, drawing to his side, to him did say,
'This morning gives us promise of a glorious day.'

A gentle answer did the Old Man make,
In courteous speech which forth he slowly drew:
And him with further words I thus bespake,
'What kind of work is that which you pursue?
This is a lonesome place for one like you.'
He answered me with pleasure and surprize;
And there was, while he spake, a fire about his eyes.

His words came feebly, from a feeble chest,
100 Yet each in solemn order followed each,
With something of a lofty utterance drest;
Choice word, and measured phrase; above the reach
Of ordinary men; a stately speech!
Such as grave Livers do in Scotland use,
Religious men, who give to God and Man their dues.

He told me that he to this pond had come
To gather Leeches, being old and poor:
Employment hazardous and wearisome!
And he had many hardships to endure:
110 From Pond to Pond he roamed, from moor to moor,
Housing, with God's good help, by choice or chance:
And in this way he gained an honest maintenance.

The Old Man still stood talking by my side;
But now his voice to me was like a stream
Scarce heard; nor word from word could I divide;
And the whole Body of the man did seem
Like one whom I had met with in a dream;
Or like a Man from some far region sent;
To give me human strength, and strong admonishment.

120   My former thoughts returned: the fear that kills;
The hope that is unwilling to be fed;
Cold, pain, and labour, and all fleshly ills;
And mighty Poets in their misery dead.
And now, not knowing what the Old Man had said,
My question eagerly did I renew,
'How is it that you live, and what is it you do?'

He with a smile did then his words repeat;
And said, that, gathering Leeches, far and wide
He travelled; stirring thus about his feet
130   The waters of the Ponds where they abide.
'Once I could meet with them on every side;
But they have dwindled long by slow decay;
Yet still I persevere, and find them where I may.'

While he was talking thus, the lonely place,
The Old Man's shape, and speech, all troubled me:
In my mind's eye I seemed to see him pace
About the weary moors continually,
Wandering about alone and silently.
While I these thoughts within myself pursued,
140   He, having made a pause, the same discourse renewed.

And soon with this he other matter blended,
Cheerfully uttered, with demeanour kind,
But stately in the main; and, when he ended,
I could have laughed myself to scorn, to find
In that decrepit Man so firm a mind.
'God,' said I, 'be my help and stay secure;
I'll think of the Leech-gatherer on the lonely moor.'

'I grieved for Buonaparte'

I grieved for Buonaparte, with a vain
And an unthinking grief! the vital blood
Of that Man's mind what can it be? What food
Fed his first hopes? What knowledge could *He* gain?
'Tis not in battles that from youth we train
The Governor who must be wise and good,
And temper with the sternness of the brain
Thoughts motherly, and meek as womanhood.
Wisdom doth live with children round her knees:
10   Books, leisure, perfect freedom, and the talk
Man holds with week-day man in the hourly walk
Of the mind's business: these are the degrees
By which true Sway doth mount; this is the stalk
True Power doth grow on; and her rights are these.

'The world is too much with us'

The world is too much with us; late and soon,
Getting and spending, we lay waste our powers:
Little we see in nature that is ours;
We have given our hearts away, a sordid boon!
This Sea that bares her bosom to the moon;
The Winds that will be howling at all hours
And are up-gathered now like sleeping flowers;
For this, for every thing, we are out of tune;
It moves us not—Great God! I'd rather be
10   A Pagan suckled in a creed outworn;
So might I, standing on this pleasant lea,
Have glimpses that would make me less forlorn;
Have sight of Proteus coming from the sea;
Or hear old Triton blow his wreathed horn.

'Methought I saw the footsteps of a throne'

Methought I saw the footsteps of a throne
Which mists and vapours from mine eyes did shroud,
Nor view of him who sate thereon allowed;
But all the steps and ground about were strown
With sights the ruefullest that flesh and bone
Ever put on; a miserable crowd,
Sick, hale, old, young, who cried before that cloud,
'Thou art our king, O Death! to thee we groan.'
I seemed to mount those steps; the vapours gave
10   Smooth way; and I beheld the face of one
Sleeping alone within a mossy cave,
With her face up to heaven; that seemed to have
Pleasing remembrance of a thought foregone;
A lovely Beauty in a summer grave!

'It is a beauteous Evening, calm and free'

It is a beauteous Evening, calm and free;
The holy time is quiet as a Nun
Breathless with adoration; the broad sun
Is sinking down in its tranquillity;
The gentleness of heaven is on the Sea:
Listen! the mighty Being is awake
And doth with his eternal motion make
A sound like thunder—everlastingly.
Dear Child! dear Girl! that walkest with me here,
10   If thou appear'st untouched by solemn thought,
Thy nature is not therefore less divine:
Thou liest in Abraham's bosom all the year;
And worshipp'st at the Temple's inner shrine,
God being with thee when we know it not.

Composed Upon Westminster Bridge

SEPT. 2, 1802

Earth has not any thing to shew more fair:
Dull would he be of soul who could pass by
A sight so touching in its majesty:
This City now doth like a garment wear
The beauty of the morning; silent, bare,
Ships, towers, domes, theatres, and temples lie
Open unto the fields, and to the sky;
All bright and glittering in the smokeless air.
Never did sun more beautifully steep
10   In his first splendor valley, rock, or hill;
Ne'er saw I, never felt, a calm so deep!
The river glideth at his own sweet will:
Dear God! the very houses seem asleep;
And all that mighty heart is lying still!

London

1802

Milton! thou should'st be living at this hour:
England hath need of thee: she is a fen
Of stagnant waters: altar, sword and pen,
Fireside, the heroic wealth of hall and bower,
Have forfeited their ancient English dower
Of inward happiness. We are selfish men;
Oh! raise us up, return to us again;
And give us manners, virtue, freedom, power.

Thy soul was like a Star and dwelt apart:
10   Thou hadst a voice whose sound was like the sea;
Pure as the naked heavens, majestic, free,
So didst thou travel on life's common way,
In cheerful godliness; and yet thy heart
The lowliest duties on itself did lay.

'Nuns fret not at their Convent's narrow room'

Nuns fret not at their Convent's narrow room;
And Hermits are contented with their Cells;
And Students with their pensive Citadels:
Maids at the Wheel, the Weaver at his Loom,
Sit blithe and happy; Bees that soar for bloom,
High as the highest Peak of Furness Fells,
Will murmur by the hour in Foxglove bells:
In truth, the prison, unto which we doom
Ourselves, no prison is: and hence to me,
10   In sundry moods, 'twas pastime to be bound
Within the Sonnet's scanty plot of ground:
Pleased if some Souls (for such there needs must be)
Who have felt the weight of too much liberty,
Should find short solace there, as I have found.

The Small Celandine

There is a Flower, the Lesser Celandine,
That shrinks, like many more, from cold and rain;
And, the first moment that the sun may shine,
Bright as the sun itself, 'tis out again!

When hailstones have been falling swarm on swarm,
Or blasts the green field and the trees distressed,
Oft have I seen it muffled up from harm,
In close self-shelter, like a Thing at rest.

But lately, one rough day, this Flower I passed,
10   And recognized it, though an altered Form,
Now standing forth an offering to the Blast,
And buffetted at will by Rain and Storm.

I stopped, and said with inly muttered voice,
'It doth not love the shower, nor seek the cold:
This neither is its courage not its choice,
But its necessity in being old.

The sunshine may not bless it, nor the dew;
It cannot help itself in its decay;
Stiff in its members, withered, changed of hue.'
20   And, in my spleen, I smiled that it was grey.

To be a Prodigal's Favorite—then, worse truth,
A Miser's Pensioner—behold our lot!
O Man! that from thy fair and shining youth
Age might but take the things Youth needed not!

'She was a Phantom of delight'

She was a Phantom of delight
When first she gleamed upon my sight;
A lovely Apparition, sent
To be a moment's ornament;
Her eyes as stars of Twilight fair;
Like Twilight's, too, her dusky hair;
But all things else about her drawn
From May-time and the cheerful Dawn;
A dancing Shape, an Image gay,
10 To haunt, to startle, and way-lay.

I saw her upon nearer view,
A Spirit, yet a Woman too!
Her household motions light and free,
And steps of virgin liberty;
A countenance in which did meet
Sweet records, promises as sweet;
A Creature not too bright or good
For human nature's daily food;
For transient sorrows, simple wiles,
20 Praise, blame, love, kisses, tears, and smiles.

And now I see with eye serene
The very pulse of the machine;
A Being breathing thoughtful breath;
A Traveller betwixt life and death;
The reason firm, the temperate will,
Endurance, foresight, strength and skill;
A perfect Woman; nobly planned,
To warn, to comfort, and command;
And yet a Spirit still, and bright
30 With something of an angel light.

October

1803

One might believe that natural miseries
Had blasted France, and made of it a land
Unfit for Men; and that in one great Band
Her Sons were bursting forth, to dwell at ease.
But 'tis a chosen soil, where sun and breeze
Shed gentle favors; rural works are there;
And ordinary business without care;
Spot rich in all things that can soothe and please!
How piteous then that there should be such dearth
10 Of knowledge; that whole myriads should unite
To work against themselves such fell despite:
Should come in phrenzy and in drunken mirth,
Impatient to put out the only light
Of Liberty that yet remains on Earth!

Ode to Duty

Stern Daughter of the Voice of God!
O Duty! if that name thou love
Who art a Light to guide, a Rod
To check the erring, and reprove;
Thou who art victory and law
When empty terrors overawe;
From vain temptations dost set free;
From strife and from despair; a glorious ministry.
There are who ask not if thine eye
10 Be on them; who, in love and truth,

Where no misgiving is, rely
Upon the genial sense of youth:
Glad Hearts! without reproach or blot;
Who do thy work, and know it not:
May joy be theirs while life shall last!
And Thou, if they should totter, teach them to stand
    fast!

Serene will be our days and bright,
And happy will our nature be,
When love is an unerring light,
20 And joy its own security.
And blessed are they who in the main
This faith, even now, do entertain:
Live in the spirit of this creed;
Yet find that other strength, according to their need.

I, loving freedom, and untried;
No sport of every random gust,
Yet being to myself a guide,
Too blindly have reposed my trust:
Resolved that nothing e'er should press
30 Upon my present happiness,
I shoved unwelcome tasks away;
But thee I now would serve more strictly, if I may.

Through no disturbance of my soul,
Or strong compunction in me wrought,
I supplicate for thy control;
But in the quietness of thought:
Me this unchartered freedom tires;
I feel the weight of chance desires:
My hopes no more must change their name,
40 I long for a repose which ever is the same.

Yet not the less would I throughout
Still act according to the voice
Of my own wish; and feel past doubt
That my submissiveness was choice:
Not seeking in the school of pride
For 'precepts over dignified,'
Denial and restraint I prize
No farther than they breed a second Will more wise.

Stern Lawgiver! yet thou dost wear
50   The Godhead's most benignant grace;
Nor know we any thing so fair
As is the smile upon thy face;
Flowers laugh before thee on their beds;
And fragrance in thy footing treads;
Thou dost preserve the Stars from wrong;
And the most ancient Heavens through Thee
   are fresh and strong.

To humbler functions, awful Power!
I call thee: I myself commend
Unto thy guidance from this hour;
60   Oh! let my weakness have an end!
Give unto me, made lowly wise,
The spirit of self-sacrifice;
The confidence of reason give;
And in the light of truth thy Bondman let me live!

Ode

Paulò majora canamus.

There was a time when meadow, grove, and stream,
The earth, and every common sight,
                    To me did seem
                Apparelled in celestial light,
The glory and the freshness of a dream.
It is not now as it has been of yore;—
                Turn wheresoe'er I may,
                    By night or day,
The things which I have seen I now can see no more.

10   The Rainbow comes and goes,
                And lovely is the Rose,
                The Moon doth with delight
        Look round her when the heavens are bare;
                Waters on a starry night
                Are beautiful and fair;
        The sunshine is a glorious birth;
        But yet I know, where'er I go,
That there hath passed away a glory from the earth.

Now, while the Birds thus sing a joyous song,
20   And while the young Lambs bound
                As to the tabor's sound,
To me alone there came a thought of grief:
A timely utterance gave that thought relief,
                And I again am strong.
The Cataracts blow their trumpets from the steep,
No more shall grief of mine the season wrong;
I hear the Echoes through the mountains throng,

The Winds come to me from the fields of sleep,
And all the earth is gay,
30   Land and sea
Give themselves up to jollity,
And with the heart of May
Doth every Beast keep holiday,
Thou Child of Joy
Shout round me, let me hear thy shouts, thou happy
Shepherd Boy!

Ye blessed Creatures, I have heard the call
Ye to each other make; I see
The heavens laugh with you in your jubilee;
My heart is at your festival,
40   My head hath its coronal,
The fullness of your bliss, I feel—I feel it all.
Oh evil day! if I were sullen
While the Earth herself is adorning,
This sweet May-morning,
And the Children are pulling,
On every side,
In a thousand vallies far and wide,
Fresh flowers; while the sun shines warm,
And the Babe leaps up on his mother's arm:—
50   I hear, I hear, with joy I hear!
—But there's a Tree, of many one,
A single Field which I have looked upon,
Both of them speak of something that is gone:
The Pansy at my feet
Doth the same tale repeat:
Whither is fled the visionary gleam?
Where is it now, the glory and the dream?

Our birth is but a sleep and a forgetting:
The Soul that rises with us, our life's Star
60   Hath had elsewhere its setting,
               And cometh from afar:
          Not in entire forgetfulness,
          And not in utter nakedness,
But trailing clouds of glory do we come
               From God, who is our home:
Heaven lies about us in our infancy!
Shades of the prison-house begin to close
            Upon the growing Boy,
But He beholds the light, and whence it flows,
70   He sees it in his joy;
The Youth, who daily farther from the East
        Must travel, still is Nature's Priest,
          And by the vision splendid
          Is on his way attended;
At length the Man perceives it die away,
And fade into the light of common day.

Earth fills her lap with pleasures of her own;
Yearnings she hath in her own natural kind,
And, even with something of a Mother's mind,
80   And no unworthy aim,
     The homely Nurse doth all she can
To make her Foster-child, her Inmate Man,
     Forget the glories he hath known,
And that imperial palace whence he came.

Behold the Child among his new-born blisses,
A four year's Darling of a pigmy size!
See, where 'mid work of his own hand he lies,
Fretted by sallies of his Mother's kisses,
With light upon him from his Father's eyes!

90   See, at his feet, some little plan or chart,
Some fragment from his dream of human life,
Shaped by himself with newly-learned art;
      A wedding or a festival,
      A mourning or a funeral;
        And this hath now his heart,
      And unto this he frames his song:
        Then will he fit his tongue
To dialogues of business, love, or strife;
      But it will not be long
100   Ere this be thrown aside,
      And with new joy and pride
The little Actor cons another part,
Filling from time to time his 'humorous stage'
With all the Persons, down to palsied Age,
That Life brings with her in her Equipage;
      As if his whole vocation
      Were endless imitation.

Thou, whose exterior semblance doth belie
      Thy Soul's immensity;
110   Thou best Philosopher, who yet dost keep
Thy heritage, thou Eye among the blind,
That, deaf and silent, read'st the eternal deep,
Haunted for ever by the eternal mind, —
      Mighty Prophet! Seer blest!
      On whom those truths do rest,
Which we are toiling all our lives to find;
Thou, over whom thy Immortality
Broods like the Day, a Master o'er a Slave,
A Presence which is not to be put by;
120   To whom the grave
Is but a lonely bed without the sense or sight
      Of day or the warm light,

A place of thought where we in waiting lie;
Thou little Child, yet glorious in the might
Of untamed pleasures, on thy Being's height,
Why with such earnest pains dost thou provoke
The Years to bring the inevitable yoke,
Thus blindly with thy blessedness at strife?
Full soon thy Soul shall have her earthly freight,
130 And custom lie upon thee with a weight,
Heavy as frost, and deep almost as life!

                O joy! that in our embers
                Is something that doth live,
                That nature yet remembers
                What was so fugitive!
The thought of our past years in me doth breed
Perpetual benedictions: not indeed
For that which is most worthy to be blest;
Delight and liberty, the simple creed
140 Of Childhood, whether fluttering or at rest,
With new-born hope for ever in his breast:—
                Not for these I raise
                The song of thanks and praise;
            But for those obstinate questionings
            Of sense and outward things,
            Fallings from us, vanishings;
            Blank misgivings of a Creature
Moving about in worlds not realized,
High instincts, before which our mortal Nature
150 Did tremble like a guilty Thing surprized:
            But for those first affections,
            Those shadowy recollections,
                Which, be they what they may,
Are yet the fountain light of all our day,
Are yet a master light of all our seeing;

Uphold us, cherish us, and make
Our noisy years seem moments in the being
Of the eternal Silence: truths that wake,
        To perish never;
160 Which neither listlessness, nor mad endeavour,
        Nor Man nor Boy,
Nor all that is at enmity with joy,
Can utterly abolish or destroy!
    Hence, in a season of calm weather,
        Though inland far we be,
Our Souls have sight of that immortal sea
        Which brought us hither,
        Can in a moment travel thither
And see the Children sport upon the shore,
170 And hear the mighty waters rolling evermore.

Then, sing ye Birds, sing, sing a joyous song!
        And let the young Lambs bound
        As to the tabor's sound!
    We in thought will join your throng,
        Ye that pipe and ye that play,
        Ye that through your hearts today
        Feel the gladness of the May!
What though the radiance which was once so bright
Be now for ever taken from my sight,
180   Though nothing can bring back the hour
Of splendour in the grass, of glory in the flower;
        We will grieve not, rather find
        Strength in what remains behind,
        In the primal sympathy
        Which having been must ever be,
        In the soothing thoughts that spring
        Out of human suffering,
        In the faith that looks through death,
In years that bring the philosophic mind.

190 And oh ye Fountains, Meadows, Hills, and Groves,
   Think not of any severing of our loves!
   Yet in my heart of hearts I feel your might;
   I only have relinquished one delight
   To live beneath your more habitual sway.
   I love the Brooks which down their channels fret,
   Even more than when I tripped lightly as they;
   The innocent brightness of a new-born Day
       Is lovely yet;
   The Clouds that gather round the setting sun
200 Do take a sober colouring from an eye
   That hath kept watch o'er man's mortality;
   Another race hath been, and other palms are won.
   Thanks to the human heart by which we live,
   Thanks to its tenderness, its joys, and fears,
   To me the meanest flower that blows can give
   Thoughts that do often lie too deep for tears.

'I wandered lonely as a Cloud'

I wandered lonely as a Cloud
That floats on high o'er Vales and Hills,
When all at once I saw a crowd
A host of dancing Daffodils;
Along the Lake, beneath the trees,
Ten thousand dancing in the breeze.

The waves beside them danced, but they
Outdid the sparkling waves in glee:—
A Poet could not but be gay
10 In such a laughing company:
I gazed—and gazed—but little thought
What wealth the shew to me had brought:

For oft when on my couch I lie
In vacant or in pensive mood,
They flash upon that inward eye
Which is the bliss of solitude,
And then my heart with pleasure fills,
And dances with the Daffodils.

Stepping Westward

While my Fellow-traveller and I were walking by the side of Loch
Ketterine, one fine evening after sun-set, in our road to a Hut where in
the course of our Tour we had been hospitably entertained some weeks
before, we met, in one of the loneliest parts of that solitary region, two
well-dressed Women, one of whom said to us, by way of greeting, 'What
you are stepping westward?'

> *'What you are stepping westward?'* — 'Yea'
> —'Twould be a wildish destiny,
> If we, who thus together roam
> In a strange Land, and far from home,
> Were in this place the guests of Chance:
> Yet who would stop, or fear to advance,
> Though home or shelter he had none,
> With such a Sky to lead him on?
>
> The dewy ground was dark and cold;
> 10   Behind, all gloomy to behold;
> And stepping westward seemed to be
> A kind of *heavenly* destiny;
> I liked the greeting; 'twas a sound
> Of something without place or bound;
> And seemed to give me spiritual right
> To travel through that region bright.
>
> The voice was soft, and she who spake
> Was walking by her native Lake:
> The salutation had to me
> 20   The very sound of courtesy:
> Its power was felt; and while my eye
> Was fixed upon the glowing sky,
> The echo of the voice enwrought
> A human sweetness with the thought
> Of travelling through the world that lay
> Before me in my endless way.

The Solitary Reaper

Behold her, single in the field,
Yon solitary Highland Lass!
Reaping and singing by herself;
Stop here, or gently pass!
Alone she cuts, and binds the grain,
And sings a melancholy strain;
O listen! for the Vale profound
Is overflowing with the sound.

No Nightingale did ever chaunt
10   So sweetly to reposing bands
Of Travellers in some shady haunt,
Among Arabian Sands:
No sweeter voice was ever heard
In spring-time from the Cuckoo-bird,
Breaking the silence of the seas
Among the farthest Hebrides.

Will no one tell me what she sings?
Perhaps the plaintive numbers flow
For old, unhappy, far-off things,
20   And battles long ago:
Or is it some more humble lay,
Familiar matter of today?
Some natural sorrow, loss, or pain,
That has been, and may be again!

Whate'er the theme, the Maiden sang
As if her song could have no ending;
I saw her singing at her work,
And o'er the sickle bending;

I listened till I had my fill:
30 And, as I mounted up the hill,
The music in my heart I bore,
Long after it was heard no more.

Elegiac Stanzas

SUGGESTED BY A PICTURE OF PEELE CASTLE, IN A
STORM, PAINTED BY SIR GEORGE BEAUMONT

I was thy Neighbour once, thou rugged Pile!
Four summer weeks I dwelt in sight of thee:
I saw thee every day; and all the while
Thy Form was sleeping on a glassy sea.

So pure the sky, so quiet was the air!
So like, so very like, was day to day!
Whene'er I looked, thy Image still was there;
It trembled, but it never passed away,

How perfect was the calm! it seemed no sleep;
10 No mood, which season takes away, or brings:
I could have fancied that the mighty Deep
Was even the gentlest of all gentle Things.

Ah! THEN, if mine had been the Painter's hand,
To express what then I saw; and add the gleam,
The light that never was, on sea or land,
The consecration, and the Poet's dream;

I would have planted thee, thou hoary Pile!
Amid a world how different from this!
Beside a sea that could not cease to smile;
20   On tranquil land, beneath a sky of bliss:

Thou shouldst have seemed a treasure-house, a mine
Of peaceful years; a chronicle of heaven:—
Of all the sunbeams that did ever shine
The very sweetest had to thee been given.

A Picture had it been of lasting ease,
Elysian quiet, without toil or strife;
No motion but the moving tide, a breeze,
Or merely silent Nature's breathing life.

Such, in the fond delusion of my heart,
30   Such Picture would I at that time have made:
And seen the soul of truth in every part;
A faith, a trust, that could not be betrayed.

So once it would have been,—'tis so no more;
I have submitted to a new control:
A power is gone, which nothing can restore;
A deep distress hath humanized my Soul.

Not for a moment could I now behold
A smiling sea and be what I have been:
The feeling of my loss will ne'er be old;
40   This, which I know, I speak with mind serene.

Then, Beaumont, Friend! who would have been the
    Friend,
If he had lived, of Him whom I deplore,
This Work of thine I blame not, but commend;
This sea in anger, and the dismal shore.

Oh 'tis a passionate Work!—yet wise and well;
Well chosen is the spirit that is here;
That Hulk which labours in the deadly swell,
This rueful sky, this pageantry of fear!

And this huge Castle, standing here sublime,
50 I love to see the look with which it braves,
Cased in the unfeeling armour of old time,
The light'ning, the fierce wind, and trampling waves.

Farewell, farewell the Heart that lives alone,
Housed in a dream, at distance from the Kind!
Such happiness, wherever it be known,
Is to be pitied; for 'tis surely blind.

But welcome fortitude, and patient cheer,
And frequent sights of what is to be borne!
Such sights, or worse, as are before me here. —
60 Not without hope we suffer and we mourn.

Lines

COMPOSED AT GRASMERE, DURING A WALK, ONE
EVENING, AFTER A STORMY DAY, THE AUTHOR HAVING
JUST READ IN A NEWSPAPER THAT THE DISSOLUTION OF
MR FOX WAS HOURLY EXPECTED

Loud is the Vale! the Voice is up
With which she speaks when storms are gone,
A mighty Unison of streams!
Of all her Voices, One!

Loud is the Vale;—this inland Depth
In peace is roaring like the Sea;
Yon Star upon the mountain-top
Is listening quietly.

Sad was I, ev'n to pain depressed,
10   Importunate and heavy load!
The Comforter hath found me here,
Upon this lonely road;

And many thousands now are sad,
Wait the fulfilment of their fear;
For He must die who is their Stay,
Their Glory disappear.

A Power is passing from the earth
To breathless Nature's dark abyss;
But when the Mighty pass away
20   What is it more than this,

That Man, who is from God sent forth,
Doth yet again to God return?—
Such ebb and flow must ever be,
Then wherefore should we mourn?

Thought of a Briton on the Subjugation of Switzerland

Two voices are there; one is of the Sea,
One of the Mountains; each a mighty Voice:
In both from age to age Thou didst rejoice,
They were thy chosen Music, Liberty!
There came a Tyrant, and with holy glee
Thou fought'st against Him; but hast vainly striven;
Thou from thy Alpine Holds at length art driven,
Where not a torrent murmurs heard by thee.
Of one deep bliss thine ear hath been bereft:
10   Then cleave, O cleave to that which still is left!
For, high-souled Maid, what sorrow would it be
That mountain Floods should thunder as before,
And Ocean bellow from his rocky shore,
And neither awful Voice be heard by thee!

St Paul's

Pressed with conflicting thoughts of love and fear
I parted from thee, Friend! and took my way
Through the great City, pacing with an eye
Downcast, ear sleeping, and feet masterless
That were sufficient guide unto themselves,
And step by step went pensively. Now, mark!
Not how my trouble was entirely hushed,
(That might not be) but how by sudden gift,
Gift of Imagination's holy power,
10 My soul in her uneasiness received
An anchor of stability. It chanced
That while I thus was pacing I raised up
My heavy eyes and instantly beheld,
Saw at a glance in that familiar spot,
A visionary scene—a length of street
Laid open in its morning quietness,
Deep, hollow, unobstructed, vacant, smooth,
And white with winter's purest white, as fair,
As fresh and spotless as he ever sheds
20 On field or mountain. Moving Form was none
Save here and there a shadowy Passenger,
Slow, shadowy, silent, dusky, and beyond
And high above this winding length of street,
This noiseless and unpeopled avenue,
Pure, silent, solemn, beautiful, was seen
The huge majestic Temple of St Paul
In awful sequestration, through a veil,
Through its own sacred veil of falling snow.

Characteristics of a Child
three Years old

Loving she is, and tractable, though wild;
And Innocence hath privilege in her
To dignify arch looks and laughing eyes;
And feats of cunning; and the pretty round
Of trespasses, affected to provoke
Mock-chastisement and partnership in play.
And, as a faggot sparkles on the hearth,
Not less if unattended and alone
Than when both young and old sit gathered round
10   And take delight in its activity,
Even so this happy Creature of herself
Is all sufficient: solitude to her
Is blithe society, who fills the air
With gladness and involuntary songs.
Light are her sallies as the tripping Fawn's
Forth-startled from the fern where she lay couched;
Unthought-of, unexpected as the stir
Of the soft breeze ruffling the meadow flowers;
Or from before it chasing wantonly
20   The many-coloured images impressed
Upon the bosom of a placid lake.

'Surprized by joy—impatient as the Wind'

Surprized by joy—impatient as the Wind
I wished to share the transport—Oh! with whom
But Thee, long buried in the silent Tomb,
That spot which no vicissitude can find?
Love, faithful love recalled thee to my mind—
But how could I forget thee!—Through what power
Even for the least division of an hour,
Have I been so beguiled as to be blind
To my most grievous loss?—That thought's return
10 Was the worst pang that sorrow ever bore,
Save one, one only, when I stood forlorn,
Knowing my heart's best treasure was no more;
That neither present time, nor years unborn
Could to my sight that heavenly face restore.

The River Duddon

CONCLUSION

I thought of Thee, my partner and my guide,
As being past away. —Vain sympathies!
For, *backward*, Duddon! as I cast my eyes,
I see what was, and is, and will abide;
Still glides the Stream, and shall for ever glide;
The Form remains, the Function never dies;

While *we*, the brave, the mighty, and the wise,
We Men, who in our morn of youth defied
The elements, must vanish;—be it so!
10 Enough, if something from our hands have power
To live, and act, and serve the future hour;
And if, as tow'rd the silent tomb we go,
Thro' love, thro' hope, and faith's transcendent dower,
We feel that we are greater than we know.

Mutability

From low to high doth dissolution climb,
And sinks from high to low, along a scale
Of awful notes, whose concord shall not fail;
A musical but melancholy chime,
Which they can hear who meddle not with crime,
Nor avarice, nor over-anxious care.
Truth fails not; but her outward forms that bear
The longest date do melt like frosty rime,
That in the morning whitened hill and plain
10 And is no more; drop like the tower sublime
Of yesterday, which royally did wear
Its crown of weeds, but could not even sustain
Some casual shout that broke the silent air,
Or the unimaginable touch of Time.

'Scorn not the Sonnet'

Scorn not the Sonnet; Critic, you have frowned,
Mindless of its just honours;—with this Key
Shakespeare unlocked his heart; the melody
Of this small Lute gave ease to Petrarch's wound;
A thousand times this Pipe did Tasso sound;
Camöens soothed with it an Exile's grief;
The Sonnet glittered a gay myrtle Leaf
Amid the cypress with which Dante crowned
His visionary brow: a glow-worm Lamp,
10   It cheered mild Spenser, called from Faery-land
To struggle through dark ways; and when a damp
Fell round the path of Milton, in his hand
The Thing became a Trumpet, whence he blew
Soul-animating strains—alas, too few!

Extempore Effusion Upon the Death of James Hogg

When first, descending from the moorlands,
I saw the Stream of Yarrow glide
Along a bare and open valley,
The Ettrick Shepherd was my guide.

When last along its banks I wandered,
Through groves that had begun to shed
Their golden leaves upon the pathways,
My steps the border minstrel led.

The mighty Minstrel breathes no longer,
10   'Mid mouldering ruins low he lies;
And death upon the braes of Yarrow,
Has closed the Shepherd-poet's eyes:

Nor has the rolling year twice measured,
From sign to sign, its stedfast course,
Since every mortal power of Coleridge
Was frozen at its marvellous source;

The rapt One, of the godlike forehead,
The heaven-eyed creature sleeps in earth:
And Lamb, the frolic and the gentle,
20   Has vanished from his lonely hearth.

Like clouds that rake the mountain-summits,
Or waves that own no curbing hand,
How fast has brother followed brother,
From sunshine to the sunless land!

Yet I, whose lids from infant slumbers
Were earlier raised, remain to hear
A timid voice, that asks in whispers,
'Who next will drop and disappear?'

Our haughty life is crowned with darkness,
30   Like London with its own black wreath,
On which with thee, O Crabbe! forth-looking,
I gazed from Hampstead's breezy heath.

As if but yesterday departed,
Thou too art gone before; but why,
O'er ripe fruit, seasonably gathered,
Should frail survivors heave a sigh?

Mourn rather for that holy Spirit,
Sweet as the spring, as ocean deep;
For Her who, ere her summer faded,
40 Has sunk into a breathless sleep.

No more of old romantic sorrows,
For slaughtered Youth or love-lorn Maid!
With sharper grief is Yarrow smitten,
And Ettrick mourns with her their Poet dead.

Notes

A Night-Piece

Wordsworth's sister, Dorothy, recorded in her journal the circumstances that inspired this poem: *The sky spread over with one continuous cloud, whitened by the light of the moon, which, though her dim shape was seen, did not throw forth so strong a light as to chequer the earth with shadows. At once the clouds seemed to cleave asunder, and left her in the centre of a black-blue vault.* (25 January 1798) Compare the above with Wordworth's poem and notice the way in which words and phrases are echoed in the latter.

See pp. 130–31 of the Approaches section for a discussion of the presentation of nature within this poem.

Does the mood established in lines 20–23 come as a surprise to you after the dramatic build up in the main body of the poem, or do you consider the *deep joy* and *peaceful calm* to be an appropriate emotional response to the scene described?

Lines Written at a Small Distance from my House

This poem celebrates spring and puts great emphasis on the relationship between man and nature. The ideas introduced here are fundamental to many of Wordsworth's later poems, including *Tintern Abbey*.

13 **Edward** Basil Montagu, son of a friend.
15–16 *Expostulation and Reply* and *The Tables Turned* also deal with the value of books as a source of wisdom.

Goody Blake and Harry Gill

In his Advertisement to *Lyrical Ballads* Wordsworth writes, *The tale of Goody Blake and Harry Gill is founded on a well-authenticated fact that happened in Warwickshire.*

'A whirl-blast from behind the hill'

In this poem Wordsworth describes a time when, while sheltering from a storm, he witnessed hailstones bombarding the dry leaves around him. Why does the poet attach importance to that particular incident?

21   **Robin Good-fellow**   a mischievous elf.

The Idiot Boy

The caring relationship that exists between Betty Foy, her son Johnny and their neighbour, Susan Gale, is a central concern in the poem. The presentation of Johnny has given rise to some controversy. Coleridge, in chapter XVII of his *Biographia Literaria* (1817) – see p. 154 for further details of this publication – while acknowledging *The Idiot Boy* to be *a fine poem*, expressed sympathy with the view that the poet had not *taken sufficient care to preclude from the reader's fancy the disgusting images of ordinary morbid idiocy, which yet it was by no means his intention to represent.* Wordsworth defended his presentation of the poem's central figure in a letter to John Wilson (7 June 1802) in which he wrote that feelings of *loathing and disgust* which many people have at the sight of an Idiot reflected *a certain want of comprehensiveness of thinking and feeling.* In that same letter Wordsworth referred to families *in the lower classes of society* where Idiots are accepted within caring relationships of the kind outlined in the poem. Wordsworth also commented *The Boy whom I had in my mind was by no means disgusting in his appearance quite the contrary and I have known several with imperfect faculties who are handsome in their persons and features.*

Some have argued that Wordsworth's deliberate move in this poem away from the artificial poetic language that was being used by many of his contemporaries takes the form of a triviality of expression that has little to recommend it. Others have viewed the plain colloquial language as a strength.

Anecdote for Fathers

Here, as in the following poem *We Are Seven*, we see the adult poet questioning a young child. In this particular case the five-year-old child is pressed by the adult to give reasons for preferring a place visited the previous year to their present location. See pp. 140–41 for further comments on this poem.

Is this poem in your view a joke by Wordsworth against Wordsworth, or do you read it in a more serious vein?

10 **Kilve** a place by the sea in Somerset where they had been the spring before.
52 **vane** weather-cock.

We Are Seven

A conversation between poet and child reveals two sharply contrasting views on death. The child relates two deaths in her family without fear or sorrow and the poet appears to be rather shocked by her careless attitude. What aspects of tone and rhythm reveal the poet's irritation in the final verses?

This poem does not suggest that one view is right and the other wrong – but it is the child's lack of awareness that appears particularly touching. The little girl possesses an *intimation of immortality*: see note on *Ode* (p. 117) for a discussion of this idea. The poet's concern here is with the nature of childhood and the gap between the child's view of life and the perspective held by the mature adult. The theme is introduced conversationally in the opening verse of the poem.

An indication of the criticism that has been levelled against the stance that Wordsworth adopts in this poem is found in Max Beerbohm's cartoon entitled 'Wordsworth in the Lake District, at Cross-Purposes' which depicts the elderly poet standing in the rain accosting a young girl. (See p. 170.)

5 **cottage girl** a girl from a rural labouring background.
47 **porringer** bowl.

Expostulation and Reply

The speaker in the second half of this poem is defending his decision to spend time away from his studies contemplating nature. What is Wordsworth's attitude towards nature in this poem? Here, and in the following poem *The Tables Turned*, Wordsworth is emphasizing the wisdom which he believed could be gained from direct contact with nature.

13 **Esthwaite lake** a small lake near Hawkshead in Cumbria which Wordsworth visited frequently during the period when he attended the Grammar School (1779–1787).
15 **Matthew** this is generally acknowledged to be a reference to William Taylor, headmaster of Hawkshead Grammar School from 1782 to 1786, who encouraged Wordsworth in his interest in poetry.
24 **wise passiveness** a state of contemplation that benefits the mind.

The Tables Turned

This poem expands the argument for learning from nature. (See also *Expostulation and Reply*.) Book learning is viewed as a poor substitute for the revelations of nature.

13 **throstle** thrush.
21 **vernal** spring-time.
25 **lore** learning.
30 **barren leaves** the leaves of the book are *barren* in comparison to the riches offered by nature.

Lines written a few miles above Tintern Abbey

This poem charts Wordsworth's developing attitude to nature. By going back into his past, recalling a period five years previously, Wordsworth reflects on how the past has influenced the present and outlines how he sees the present in its turn having an influence on the future.

See pp. 132–5 for activities and discussion arising from a close reading of this poem. In the notes Wordsworth dictated to his friend Isabella Fenwick he made the following comments: *No poem of mine was composed under circumstances more pleasant for me to remember than this. I began it upon leaving Tintern, after crossing the Wye, and concluded it just as I was entering Bristol in the evening, after a ramble of 4 or 5 days, with my sister. Not a line of it was altered, and not any part of it written down till I reached Bristol.*

'A slumber did my spirit seal'

This is the first of the five Lucy poems, a group which allude to the death of a girl who is named in all but one of the poems as Lucy. 'A slumber did my spirit seal' is one of the four written in Germany in 1798–9 and then published in the 1800 edition of *Lyrical Ballads* (see also Song, 'Strange fits of passion I have known' and 'Three years she grew in sun and shower'); 'I travelled among unknown Men' first appeared in the 1807 *Poems.*

In a letter of 6 April 1799, Coleridge linked the mysterious central figure in this poem with Wordsworth's sister Dorothy. Peggy Hutchinson (Mary Wordsworth's sister), who died young in 1796, has also been mentioned in this context. But the issue of Lucy's identity does not really matter when reading the poems.

Critical discussion of this poem has focused on the relationship between the poem's two stanzas. Are these stanzas contrasting the poet's frame of mind before and after the death of his loved one and thus emphasizing the shock of her death? Or do both stanzas describe the poet's reaction to the death, therefore offering a more positive reaction to the event? Such questions point to the essential ambivalence of this poem: Wordsworth's acceptance of Lucy's death is threatened by his sense of grief for his loved one.

7   **diurnal** daily.

Song ('She dwelt among th'untrodden ways')

See note to 'A *slumber did my spirit seal*' p. 107.

A number of ambiguities exist in this poem, particularly when certain lines are taken out of context. For example, lines 3 and 4 suggest that Lucy was not a lovable or praiseworthy character. In the same way think carefully about the implications of the image in lines 7 and 8. Do you think that such ambiguity adds to or detracts from your final response to the poem?

2   **Dove** rivers of this name appear in Derbyshire, Yorkshire and Westmorland. Such uncertainty of location seems appropriate when seen within the context of the many ambiguities that appear within this poem. The name of the river also has associations with peace and beauty.

'Strange fits of passion I have known'

See note to 'A *slumber did my spirit seal*' p. 107.

The disappearance of the moon as the poet travels towards Lucy's cottage gives rise to a fear that his loved one may be dead – hence the *strange fits of passion* referred to in the opening line of the poem.

6   Comparison with a rose serves to emphasize Lucy's beauty without allowing the reader to forget that she, like the flower, will finally perish.

Lucy Gray

The following comment relating to the poem was dictated by Wordsworth and compiled by Isabella Fenwick in 1843: *founded on a circumstance told me by my sister of a little girl who, not far from Halifax in Yorkshire, was bewildered in a snowstorm. Her footsteps were traced by her parents to the middle of the lock of a canal.*

The rhythmic and rhyming patterns within this poem follow the established form of a ballad. What do you gain from Wordsworth's use of the first person? Some have argued that the strength of this poem lies in the way the poet's feelings are revealed to us. Do you agree?

Nutting

This memory of childhood was originally intended for the long autobiographical poem entitled *The Prelude*, but Wordsworth later decided that it was not needed there.

9   **frugal Dame** Ann Tyson, with whom Wordsworth lodged while attending Hawkshead School.

19   **virgin scene** the boy's act of destruction is compared to a rape. After the *ravage* (43) the nook *patiently gave up* (45) its *quiet being*(46).

41–43   Alliteration and heavy monosyllables emphasize the sudden surge of brutality.

52–54   Compare the mood of these closing lines with the buoyant opening of the poem. How does the boy's new perspective of nature differ from his previous view?

'Three years she grew in sun and shower'

See note to 'A *slumber did my spirit seal*' p. 107.

Nature's reference to taking Lucy prepares the reader for Lucy's death in the final stanza. Notice the way balanced phrases such as *sun and shower*, *law and impulse* and *rock and plain* are used to suggest the opposing forces at work in nature.

Rural Architecture

The rhythmic energy of this poem echoes Wordsworth's enthusiasm for the boys' building exploits.

4 **Great How** a hill in the Lake District.
12 **The Magog** a figure who appears in legends about Britain's early history.

Michael

Wordsworth's insertion of the phrase *pastoral poem* links this poem with a well-established literary tradition which features nostalgic views of shepherds living in carefree surroundings. Wordsworth presents Michael, the shepherd in his poem, without sentimentality; the simplicity of the narrative outlining Michael's life and misfortunes gains dignity through the movement of the blank verse.

In a letter to his friend Thomas Poole, Wordsworth describes his intentions in this poem: *I have attempted to give a picture of a man, of strong mind and lively sensibility, agitated by two of the most powerful affections of the human heart: the parental affection, and the love of property, landed property, including the feelings of inheritance, home, and personal and family independence.* (9 April 1801)

1–8   Following the opening invitation to turn from the public path brings the reader face to face with a difficult climb before finding the *hidden valley* which was once Michael's home. It has been argued that this opening provides not only local colour but also a statement of the main concern of the poem – man's struggle against the forces which finally pull him down. The same section has also been referred to as a clumsy address to the reader. What is your view of this opening?

2   **Green-head Gill** a mountain stream north of Grasmere in the Lake District.

11   **kites** at that time a common bird of prey in Britain.

17   **heap of unhewn stones** these same stones reappear in line 337.

268   **Richard Bateman** Robert (not Richard) Bateman provided money for the rebuilding of Ings Chapel in the Lake District.

334   **Sheep-fold** an unroofed building of stone walls offering shelter for sheep.

490   It seems ironic that Michael's immortality should lie in the *unfinished Sheep-fold* rather than in his son or his land.

'I travelled among unknown Men'

See note to 'A *slumber did my spirit seal*' p. 107.

The poet's experiences abroad among *unknown Men* are viewed as a *melancholy dream:* affection for England is linked with thoughts of Lucy.

11   Lucy is presented here turning a spinning wheel by the fireside.

'My heart leaps up when I behold'

The language in all but the closing line of this poem is very simple, almost childlike; however, the ideas explored here need to be thought about carefully.

2   In *Genesis* (IX: 12–17) the rainbow features as a token of the pledge that God established with mankind after the Flood. It has

been argued that a childhood in which rainbows provide a symbol of continuity has an uncomfortable sound. What do you think?

7–9 These lines were added as an epigraph to *Ode 'There was a time'* in the 1815 publication of that poem.

9 **piety** the sense of duty and love we naturally owe to our parents. Wordsworth implies that he owes similar emotions to his childhood. The parent/child role is fused in line 7.

Resolution and Independence

This poem, originally known as *The Leech Gatherer*, provides an example of the way in which Wordsworth edited sources according to the needs of his imagination. His sister Dorothy's diary entry for 3 October 1800 (two years before the poem was written) reveals that Wordsworth was not alone when he encountered the old man and that the actual meeting took place on a public road, not on a lonely moor.

The leech gatherer, who would have made his living by collecting aquatic blood-sucking worms that were used medicinally for drawing blood, does not actually appear until the eighth stanza: what are the concerns of the opening seven stanzas of the poem?

5 **Stock-dove** wood pigeon.

43 **Chatterton** a poet who committed suicide in 1770 at the age of 18.

45–46 This is a reference to Robert Burns, an eighteenth-century poet who wrote his best work while still a farmer. He died in 1796 at the age of 37.

64–72 These lines are quoted by Wordsworth in his Preface to *Poems* (1815) to illustrate the workings of his imagination. Here the old man is transformed into a dream-like figure.

141–47 What moral does Wordsworth outline in this concluding stanza?

'I grieved for Buonaparte'

Wordsworth was fired with new enthusiam for the sonnet form after hearing his sister read to him the sonnets of John Milton (1608–1674).

In 1804, two years after this poem was written, Napoleon Buonaparte proclaimed himself Emperor of France. See pp. 151–2 for details of Napoleon's military exploits and for comment on Wordsworth's reactions.

What characteristics of statesmanship is Wordsworth advocating in this sonnet?

'The world is too much with us'

The *world* Wordsworth refers to in the title of this poem is the world of practical considerations and distractions – approximately the opposite to the world of nature. Lines 5–8 offer a metaphorical presentation of aspects of nature with which Wordsworth argues we are out of tune. The final sestet presents nature through pagan mythology: Wordsworth argues that although the pagan view is *outworn*, it is at least preferable to the kind of alienation from nature that he sees in contemporary society.

3 The inversion of this line, laying stress on *little*, emphasizes a tone of indignation. What other moments in this sonnet reinforce the same tone?
13 **Proteus** an old man who received the gift of prophecy from the sea god Neptune.
14 **Triton** Neptune's son.

'Methought I saw the footsteps of a throne'

The opening echoes Milton's sonnet '*Methought I saw my late espoused saint*'.

The image of death that we are presented with in the final sestet is very different from what we are prepared for in the opening octave of this sonnet. What are the differences and what do these contrasting images imply about attitudes to death?

'It is a beauteous Evening, calm and free'

9 **Dear Child** Caroline, Wordsworth's illegitimate daughter by Annette Vallon. Wordsworth met Annette while on a visit to France; their child was born December 1792. This poem was written in 1802 when Wordsworth accompanied by Dorothy, revisited Annette and Caroline.

12 **Abraham's bosom** the final resting place of the happy after death (Luke XVI:22). This line suggests that Wordsworth is thinking of the child's development in terms that he outlined more fully in *Ode 'There was a time'*. Reread particularly lines 58–66 of that poem in which Wordsworth refers to a child's previous existence, before birth, as being close to God – an existence still remembered in childhood before the concerns of day-to-day living make such memories fade.

Composed Upon Westminster Bridge

Wordsworth views London in early morning when there is little sign of the bustle that is usually associated with city life. The personified city is seen to wear the morning beauty *like a garment*; the implication is that beneath that covering the essential ugliness is to be found. What other details of the sonnet suggest that Wordsworth's admiration for London is restricted to that moment only, not to the usual character of the place?

14 There is a suggestion here that the city is not merely sleeping but also dead, its heart stilled.

London, 1802

In a note that he dictated to Isabella Fenwick – a friend of
Wordsworth in his later years – Wordsworth commented on the
tone of this poem. He said that it was written immediately after
his return from France to London, when he was particularly taken
by the contrast between the sense of desolation that the
revolution had produced in France and the pomp and vanity that
he witnessed in London.

1   The poet John Milton (1608–1674) epitomized the qualities, as
listed in line 8, that Wordsworth wanted to see restored to society.

'Nuns fret not at their Convent's narrow room'

In a letter dated November 1802, Wordsworth wrote about
Milton's sonnets, *I think the music exceedingly well suited to its end,
that is, it has an energetic and varied flow of sound crowding into
narrow room more of the combined effect of rhyme and blank verse
than can be done by any other kind of verse I know of.*

6   **Furness Fells** a mountainous area in the south-western part of the
Lake District.

The Small Celandine

Wordsworth was fascinated by the celandine's habit of shutting
itself up and then opening out according to the degree of light
and temperature. What points does Wordsworth see in the ageing
process of the celandine that he can then relate to the
predicament of humanity?

'She was a Phantom of delight'

Each of the three stanzas of this poem presents a different view of Mary Hutchinson, Wordsworth's wife.

22 **machine** the human body viewed as a collection of many parts.

October, 1803

When this sonnet was written, Napoleon Buonaparte's invasion of England seemed imminent. See pp. 151–2 for comment on how Wordsworth's attitude towards Napoelon changed as the latter's power grew.

Ode to Duty

The opening stanza addresses a personification of duty. What details of the second and third stanzas suggest a feeling of loss as the poet outlines how some are content to live intuitively? In the fourth and fifth stanzas Wordsworth expresses his wish for more order and security. In stanza six (lines 41–48) the poet emphasizes that if he is to do his duty, it must be because it is what he wants to do – an idea that Wordsworth felt unhappy with later as indicated by the omission of this stanza in all editions after 1807.

In the closing stanzas of the poem Wordsworth makes a plea to live under the guidance of duty which he acknowledges as being a powerful organizing force within the universe.

Ode ('There was a time')

The 1807 epigraph *Paulò majora canamus* (Let us sing of somewhat more exalted things) appears at the beginning of Virgil's *Fourth Eclogue* which has been viewed as prophesying the birth of Christ and the beginning of a new age. In the 1815 publication of this ode the title was extended to *Ode: Intimations of Immortality from Recollections of Early Childhood* and the last three lines of *My heart leaps up* appeared as an epigraph to the poem. What do you see as the link between the three-line epigraph and the ode?

You may find it helpful to divide your reading of the poem into the following sections:

Stanzas 1–4 (lines 1–57)   These outline a sense of loss felt by the poet when as an adult he can no longer recollect fully the experiences he associates with childhood.

Stanzas 5–8 (lines 58–131)   Wordsworth explains the reasons for the loss of the *visionary gleam* in adulthood. He sees childhood as being close to a state of prior existence, an external force of life, links to which are weakened by the processes of living.

his loss and considers what is left to sustain him as an adult.

Wordsworth wrote the following in a letter to Catherine Clarkson in January 1815: *This poem rests entirely upon two recollections of childhood, one that of a splendour in the objects of sense which is passed away, and the other an indisposition to bend to the law of death as applying to our own particular case. A Reader who has not a vivid recollection of these feelings having existed in his mind in childhood cannot understand that poem.*

9   Is the mood established by the monosyllables in this line one of despair, acceptance or a combination of these emotions?

23   **A timely utterance** perhaps a reference to *My heart leaps up*.

41   Do you interpret the repetition of *I feel* as an emphatic statement of joy or a hesitant cry of desperation?

76   **the light of common day** this phrase contrasts with the *celestial light* (4) and *visionary gleam* (56).

82   **Inmate**   continuing the image of the *prison-house* (67).

85–89   These lines could be viewed as a sentimental presentation of childhood or as a portrayal of a remembered family scene.

110   What qualities is Wordsworth referring to when he addresses the child as *best Philosopher*? The image of the child as *Eye among the blind* (111) offers a helpful starting point.

114–116   See p. 145 for discussion of the effect achieved by these lines.

164–170   Here Wordsworth compares human development with a journey away from the source of life – a development of the metaphor introduced in line 71.

190–   In this final stanza Wordsworth outlines his resolution to the problem he confronted at the opening of the poem. Although his response to nature has changed since childhood, he finds some consolation in what adulthood has to offer. In the closing lines Wordsworth hints at having gained a new sensitivity to the thoughts and feelings of others.

'I wandered lonely as a Cloud'

Wordsworth moves from a remembered observation of an expanse of daffodils to an account of the creative process itself. See pp. 135–6 for discussion of aspects of this poem, p. 135 for an extract from Dorothy's journal which records the discovery of the wild daffodils, and p. 163 for Wordsworth's letter to George Beaumont which examines the language of the poem.

3   What effect is achieved by moving from the notion of a *crowd* to a *host* on the following line?

15–16   In his *Biographia Literaria* (ch. XXII) – see p. 154 for details of this publication – Coleridge quotes these lines as an example of Wordsworth's *mental bombast* referring to his inclusion of *thoughts and images too great for the subject*. Do you agree with this view?

16   The poet's solitary position outlined in these closing lines is very different from the state of isolation described at the opening: in the final stanza, as a result of visionary insight, the poet is alone but not lonely.

Stepping Westward

The greetings which people exchange are usually meaningless. In this poem Wordsworth encourages the reader to think again about the wording of a particular greeting emphasizing the way in which it increased his pleasure in the sunset – an obvious Romantic source of inspiration.

12 ***heavenly*** **destiny** the use of italics here emphasizes the spiritual rightness that the poet links with his journey into the sunset. The deliberate vagueness with which this phrase is introduced – *seemed to be/A kind of . . .* – is an instance of the combination of simple and more formal vocabulary that is found throughout the poem.
21 **Its power was felt** is this a reference to the power of the greeting or of the sunset? Indeed, does such an ambiguity suggest a blending of the two ideas?
26 Does this final line extend the travelling metaphor for the journey we make through life?

The Solitary Reaper

Wordsworth acknowledged that this poem was suggested to him after reading an extract from Thomas Wilkinson's *Tours to the British Mountains* (1824): *Passed a female who was reaping alone: she sung in Erse as she bended over her sickle; the sweetest human voice I ever heard: her strains were tenderly melancholy, and felt delicious, long after they were heard no more.*

Stanzas 1 and 4 are linked by a common rhyme scheme plus a concern to describe the physical circumstances of Wordsworth and the singer. A separate rhyme scheme is common to stanzas 2 and 3; what aspects are explored in these two stanzas?

12 **Arabian Sands** this reference broadens the geographical perspective of the poem. It also gives the song a mysterious, magical quality.

Elegiac Stanzas

In this poem Wordsworth points towards his changed reactions to
Peele Castle as a way of expressing his changed view of life which
has come about as the result of the loss of his brother John at sea.
The connection between Sir George Beaumont's painting of the
castle (mentioned in the epigraph) and Wordsworth's brother's
death is not at first obvious. (See p. 173.) The poem opens with
Wordsworth remembering that he once spent four summer weeks
by Peele Castle; his memories of the place are such that if he had
been a painter and had painted it, then he would have painted a
tranquil scene, very different from Beaumont's depiction of the
place in a storm. But, in the ninth stanza, the mood changes as
the poet admits that his view of life is not what it was.
Beaumont's picture now seems to hold more life than the *smiling*
scene Wordsworth has previously outlined, and he praises the
artist for painting things as they really are. The poem closes in a
mood of optimism as the poet accepts his new approach to life
with resignation. A sense of moral earnestness pervades.

There is a strong feeling of balance within the poem: the first
half is balanced against the second and phrase is balanced against
phrase. What effect is achieved by such a structure?

1   **thou rugged Pile** Peele Castle, the subject of Beaumont's
     painting stands on a rocky outcrop guarding the entrance to
     Barrow-in-Furness harbour. Wordsworth was a visitor to the
     area in 1794.

14–15   **the gleam, The light that never was** a reference to the poet's
     illusions.

16   **consecration** Some critics have suggested that the religious
     connotations of this word suggest that Wordsworth's early view
     was not all *delusion* (29). What do you think?

17   **hoary** ancient.

18   **how different from this** emphasizes the difference between
     Wordsworth's early tranquil memories of Peele Castle and the
     stormy scene depicted in Beaumont's picture.

26   **Elysian quiet** In Greek mythology Elysium is the final home of
     the blessed.

36   **deep distress** Wordsworth's grief at the death of his brother.

40 Here suffering is linked with serenity. The final stanza emphasizes this attitude of acceptance.
47 **That Hulk** In the foreground of Beaumont's painting a ship is battling in heavy seas.
53 Wordsworth rejects the solitary life.
54 **Kind** humankind.

Lines, Composed at Grasmere

Wordsworth had great respect for Charles James Fox, a Whig politician who died in 1806. What comfort, in the face of Fox's imminent death, does the poet gain in the closing stanzas of the poem?

Thought of a Briton on the Subjugation of Switzerland

The Swiss, who symbolized liberty for Wordsworth, were invaded by the French, under the leadership of Napoleon Buonaparte, in 1798. See pp. 151–2 for comment on Wordsworth's reaction to this event.

St Paul's

Wordsworth describes how early one winter morning the area around St Paul's Cathedral became transformed for him into a *visionary scene*, an unreal landscape. Through detailed description the reader is directed steadily along the urban vista leading ultimately to the veiled grandeur of the cathedral. The dash in line 15 divides the poem into two sections; the focus shifts from concern with the poet's mental unease in the first, to a description of the transformed surroundings in the second.

Look closely at the use of adjectives in the poem. The lists that appear in lines 17, 22 and 25 help to convey a sense of the unreality of the scene. In what sense do you think that Wordsworth found *An anchor of stability* in the rather ethereal vision that he decribes?

For an illustration of Wordsworth's manuscript for *St Paul's* see p. 172.

Characteristics of a Child three Years old

The child referred to here is Wordsworth's second daughter, Catherine; the poet's reactions to this same child's early death are recorded in *'Surprized by joy – impatient as the Wind.'*

At what stage in the poem do you begin to get a clear picture of the child?

5 **trespasses** wrongs.
7 **faggot** bundle of sticks.

'Surprized by joy – impatient as the Wind'

The excitement of the opening lines is soon abandoned as this sonnet is transformed into a record of the poet's grief at the long-passed death of his daughter, Catherine. The first eight-and-a-half lines express conflicting emotions; the speaker moves from one half-finished sentence to another, breaking up the lines awkwardly and thus achieving the effect of spontaneity within a very structured verse form. Compare the rapid acceleration of the opening one-and-a-half lines with the solemnity of the poem's close. Is the final note one of anger or acceptance?

2 **transport** rapturous emotion.
4 **vicissitude** change of fortune. The question mark at the end of line 4 refers back to *with whom?* Line 4 therefore becomes a statement of fact.
5 The 'poetic' language of this line contrasts with the more natural outburst which opens the next. What effect is achieved by this contrast within the poem?

The River Duddon: Conclusion

This is the last in a series of poems prompted by the River Duddon which flows into the sea in the south west of the Lake District. Wordsworth contrasts the sense of permanence associated with the river to the transitory nature of humanity. What ideas, introduced in the final five lines of the sonnet, lead to the closing note of optimism?

13   **transcendent dower** a gift excelling all others.

Mutability

In the opening lines the process of change is compared to music which produces harmonies audible only to the careful listener. A distinction is then made between the unalterable essence of things and the *outer forms* which are easily subjected to change. Two different processes of change are presented: one is compared to the melting of frost, the other to the violent collapse of a tower – the contrast between these two images is dramatic and memorable.

12   **crown of weeds** is there a note of irony here?

'Scorn not the Sonnet'

In this celebration of the sonnet Wordsworth names writers whose exploration of that poetic form he admired.

4   **Petrarch** a fourteenth-century Italian poet.
5   **Tasso** a sixteenth-century Italian poet.
6   **Camöens** a sixteenth-century Portuguese poet.
7   **myrtle** a shrub used as an emblem for love.
8   **cypress** a coniferous tree, the branches or sprigs of which symbolize mourning.

8   **Dante** an Italian poet of the early fourteenth century.
10 **Spenser** in the Sixteenth century Edmund Spenser published six out of twelve planned books of a poem entitled *The Faerie Queene.*
12 **Milton** See notes to '*I grieved for Buonaparte*' and '*Nuns fret not at their Convent's narrow room*' for comment on Wordsworth's admiration of Milton's sonnets.

Extempore Effusion Upon the Death of James Hogg

This poem was written in 1835 after Wordsworth heard of the death of James Hogg, a poet and ballad collector.

4   **Ettrick Shepherd** James Hogg, born in Ettrick Forest in Scotland and at one time a shepherd, was with Wordsworth when he first visited neighbouring Yarrow Water in 1814.
8   **border minstrel** Walter Scott, poet and novelist, accompanied Wordsworth when he returned to Yarrow Water in 1831.
10 Scott died in 1832 and was buried in the ruins of Dryburgh Abbey on the River Tweed.
11 **braes** banks.
12 **Shepherd-poet** James Hogg.
15 Coleridge died in 1834.
19 **Lamb** Charles Lamb died in 1834.
31 **Crabbe** George Crabbe, who used to visit Wordsworth in London, died in 1832.
37 **holy Spirit** Felicia Hemans died in 1835 aged 42.

Approaches

Introduction

William Wordsworth's poems have excited extreme reactions — both favourable and otherwise — ever since they were first published at the end of the eighteenth century. His literary output is vast, extremely varied and rather uneven in quality. In such a situation, sweeping generalizations about developments during Wordsworth's extended poetic career are not particularly helpful; however, a close reading of individual poems offers an important step in reaching conclusions about Wordsworth's work at different stages in his career and ultimately about his literary achievement.

Wordsworth's writing is explored below in four sections:

> Wordsworth and Nature

> Wordsworth and Childhood

> Wordsworth in his Time

> Wordsworth's Language

The first two sections isolate concerns that recur in Wordsworth's poetry. We explore what attitudes to nature are revealed in his work, and examine the ambiguities which arise from a close reading of a group of five poems that are usually known as the Lucy poems. The third section argues that knowledge of Wordsworth's early childhood development is important to an understanding of the shifting focus of his writing. In the final section Wordsworth's theories about language — particularly as stated in his revolutionary Preface to *Lyrical Ballads* — are introduced, and you will be asked to consider ways in which these theoretical concerns are reflected in Wordsworth's poems, as well as the relative success of poems in which he *ignores* his own theories about language.

Wordsworth and Nature

Nature figures prominently in many of Wordsworth's poems. The poet's attitudes towards nature and its influence on people do not, however, follow a single rigid system.

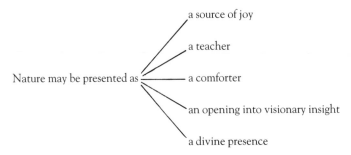

The categories above do not form a definitive list, but they should help you to start thinking about the many ways in which Wordsworth presents nature in his poems.

Activity

Read *A Night-Piece* (p. 1). What is Wordsworth's attitude towards nature in this poem?

Discussion

You may well have considered the way in which within *A Night-Piece* a sudden break in the cloud, illuminated by the moon, is described as a *vision*, an insight beyond everyday experience, which leaves the mind in *deep joy* finally giving way to *peaceful calm* and a readiness for meditation. Nature has become a doorway into a trance-like state which leads us, as suggested in *Expostulation and Reply*, into a condition of *wise passiveness*. (See note on p. 106.) The final mood is one of serenity. Within this particular poem Wordsworth has presented nature as an opening into visionary insight and as a source of joy.

Attitudes to nature, such as these in *A Night-Piece* are re-established and elaborated in later poems. '*I wandered lonely as a Cloud*' offers an interesting development. This poem follows the stages that lead the poet from observation of a display of daffodils to a consideration of the way in which such a moment will sustain him at a later date. In the opening line, *lonely as a Cloud* suggests detachment from immediate surroundings, but the appearance of the daffodils breaks that mood. The poet seems to gain pleasure and energy from the movement of the flowers and the agitated surface of the water. Indeed, his response is not limited to that particular moment; the third stanza indicates that the poet has the power to recall that experience on future occasions:

> For oft when on my couch I lie
> In vacant or in pensive mood,
> They flash upon that inward eye
> Which is the bliss of solitude,
> And then my heart with pleasure fills,
> And dances with the Daffodils. (13–18)

Here the emphasis is on the mind's ability to recollect the experience, and on the pleasure that the poet gains from that recollection.

Nature is being presented in the above lines as a comforter – one of the ideas which is explored more fully in *Lines written a few miles above Tintern Abbey*. A remarkable feature of this latter poem is Wordsworth's ability to combine close observation of the details of nature with a sense of something other than what is immediately perceptible; in long involved sentences, Wordsworth presents a passionate assessment of the value and significance of the surroundings. Although at the outset a landscape appears to be the subject of the poem, it soon becomes evident that what the poet is really concerned to describe here is the effect that such surroundings had upon his own inner life. An unravelling of the attitudes towards nature in this particular poem reveals aspects of Wordsworth's varied approach towards the subject.

Tintern Abbey

Tintern Abbey begins with the poet telling us of the occasion he is describing; he is revisiting the Wye Valley in Gwent after a gap of five years. (See illustration on p. 173.) The landscape is presented in the opening section to the extent that you can view with the poet, from his seat under the tree, the cottages, orchards and hedgerows. Visual detail is dominant, but there is also a reference to muted sound – the *murmur* of the water – that surfaces from the otherwise silent landscape. Such attention to details of landscape, although a feature of eighteenth-century topographical poetry, is not a characteristic of Wordsworth's poems. Physical particulars usually appear sparingly in a landscape that has little or no colour; here, however, from his viewing point under a *dark sycamore*, the poet catalogues the sights, and the effect is to impress on us the immediacy of the scene. Another feature of the opening is the repetition of the first person singular; in this instance (although it is not always the case in Wordsworth's poems or in poetry generally), it seems likely that we are hearing the voice of the poet himself who fills the foreground in this section of the poem.

Activity

Read lines 23–50 carefully and make notes on what Wordsworth says he owes to the memory of this landscape.

Discussion

Lines 23–50 focus attention on what the same scene meant to the poet five years ago and the effects that the memory has had on him in the intervening years. Breaking up this section of the poem into smaller units may help you to explore the details more fully. In lines 23–31 Wordsworth states that memories of this landscape offered a comfort to him when he was tired, and allowed him to enter a tranquil state of mind. In lines 31–36 it is suggested that the pleasure he gained from such landscape helped him unconsciously to shape his moral development, and in lines 36–39 memories of that same landscape are seen to be responsible for allowing him to pass, on occasions, into a *serene and blessed mood* which enables him to see beyond the superficial detail of this existence *into the life of things*, and therefore to make sense of what under normal circumstances seems to the poet *unintelligible*.

Wordsworth keeps the most important point until last; once he is transported into that state of mind he is able to see into things and to understand them completely. So now the focus of the poem has shifted from an initial concern with an actual landscape to a concentration on the way in which that landscape has affected the mind of the poet. And the language has shifted accordingly; the language of natural description has given way to the language of meditation, a state which seems to have been produced by contemplating nature. As the poem progresses it becomes clear that its real subject is not nature as seen at Tintern Abbey, but rather experiences that are open to the mind which can create and recall at will a mental landscape based on a remembered scene.

In the next short section (lines 50–58) a note of uncertainty is introduced into the poet's presentation of his ideas, and that same doubtful mood is felt in the opening of the fourth section of the poem before Wordsworth develops a comparison between his relationship with nature on his first visit to Tintern Abbey five years ago and his present state. The previous occasion was characterized by an emotional approach, but the poet has now acquired the ability to see through nature to the forces that underlie it. The final lines of this section reveal that in his present state of mind the poet is ready to see nature as

> The anchor of my purest thoughts, the nurse,
> The guide, the guardian of my heart, and soul
> Of all my moral being.   (110–112)

As you re-read *Tintern Abbey* keep these points in mind; you will see that each is touched upon elsewhere in the poem.

The final section of the poem (lines 112–160) makes reference to Wordsworth's sister, Dorothy. He sees in her the same kind of wild passionate approach to nature that he used to hold in his youth, and he airs a conviction that she will eventually share his

more meditative approach to nature. Here Wordsworth acknowledges Dorothy's potential to enter the meditative world of
abstraction that he inhabits – but he hints that a number of
years of intellectual maturity are needed before Dorothy's mind
will become *a mansion for all lovely forms*. An interesting
perspective on the rather condescending tone of these lines is
offered by John Barrell in a section of his *Poetry, Language and
Politics* (1988) entitled 'The uses of Dorothy: 'The Language of
the Sense' in *Tintern Abbey*'. There he gives evidence to support
the fact that in eighteenth-century Britain women were excluded
from what was called the 'republic of letters': such attitudes
continued through the late eighteenth century despite the fact
that at that time the potential of women – the very quality
which Wordsworth brings to our attention – was being firmly
asserted by writers of the calibre of Mary Wollstonecraft, whose
Vindication of the Rights of Woman was published in 1792.

In the closing lines of *Tintern Abbey*, the poet acknowledges
himself a *worshipper of Nature* and includes a prayer in which he
looks to the future and calls upon nature to comfort his sister in
the sorrows of life that she may have to endure.

Tintern Abbey is a detailed and complex poem. The activity
below may help you to explore your understanding of the poem.

Activity

Read *Tintern Abbey* and as you do so make a list of the attitudes
towards nature that you find in it. Think carefully about the
progression of ideas within the poem.

Discussion

Your list may be a long one which may include some of the
attitudes given on p. 130. In the final section of *Tintern Abbey* the
poem comes full circle; it begins and ends with the notion of nature
as comforter – initially in relation to the poet, and finally in relation
to his sister.

The ideas that Wordsworth explores in *Tintern Abbey* can also be found within other poems in this selection. In *Lines Written at a Small Distance from my House*, for example, he stresses the importance of the relationship between humanity and nature. In *Expostulation and Reply* he considers the influence of the *powers of* nature which have the ability to *feed this mind of ours*, and in *The Tables Turned* he develops an argument for learning from nature.

Such a mix of ideas makes it impossible to extract a simple statement on Wordsworth's attitude to nature. He does not offer a clear system or a consistent philosophy: indeed, the attitudes to nature that are found in *Tintern Abbey* alone, reveal the variety in Wordsworth's approach to this subject.

The solitary poet?

The repetition of 'I' in *Tintern Abbey* as well as emphasizing the personal perspective which is central to the poem also creates the impression that isolation is a necessary condition for the experiences described within the poem. You may remember that the poet's isolated state is a feature of '*I wandered lonely as a Cloud*' too, but in that particular instance an entry in Dorothy's journal offers a different perspective on the same occasion.

Activity

What light does the following extract from Dorothy's journal shed for you on the poem and its composition?

> *I never saw daffodils so beautiful they grew among the mossy stones about and about them, some rested their heads upon these stones as on a pillow for weariness and the rest tossed and reeled and danced and seemed as if they verily laughed with the wind that blew upon them over the lake, they looked so gay ever glancing ever changing.* (15 April 1802)

Discussion

It is obvious from Dorothy's record of the event that brother and sister were *both* present on this occasion, but Wordsworth chose to recreate the landscape in '*I wandered lonely as a Cloud*' with himself as the solitary viewer, and the effect is to emphasize the private and particular nature of the experience.

There are, however, within this selection, a number of poems in which Wordsworth describes isolated figures other than himself who appear against a distinctive rural setting. Two such poems are *Resolution and Independence* and *The Solitary Reaper*: the first features a leech gatherer, the second a girl singing in the highlands, and these figures bring attention to themselves by virtue of their position and appearance. But Wordsworth himself is also present in the poems – and in *Resolution and Independence* he is not merely an observer but also a participant in the action.

Figures in the landscape

The opening stanzas of *Resolution and Independence* describe the morning after a heavy storm. Wordsworth sets out for a walk feeling light-hearted, *as happy as a Boy*, but as the walk continues his mood changes from happiness to depression. He ponders on the fate of other poets (see p. 112 for notes on Chatterton and Burns) and thinks how easily he could suffer similar mental hardship. It is in this uneasy mood that Wordsworth encounters the leech gatherer, a mysterious old man whose being troubles the poet. The presence of this figure and the circumstances of the meeting form the core of the poem.

Activity

How does Wordsworth suggest the strangeness of the old man in lines 64–70 of *Resolution and Independence*?

Discussion

A consideration of the effect created by the combination of similes in these lines should help you to answer this question.

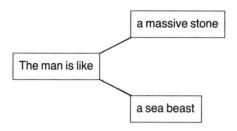

The first comparison emphasizes the old man's inert stance and the way in which he seems to be part of the natural surroundings. The second simile, in which the old man is compared to a sea beast which has crawled beside the pool to sun itself, works upon the previous image and gives it a life of its own, thus linking the old man with the animal world. Does this combination of images evoke for you a feeling of terror or of awe?

This strange being – bent double, leaning on a wooden staff – is described in line 82 as *motionless as a cloud*, a link with ethereal creations which provides a dramatic jump from the crawling sea beast cited earlier. Through such disparate images the old man's strangeness is emphasized. The poet is fascinated by what he sees. Wordsworth then questions the old man, who replies with dignity, but the content of the reply is lost on the questioner because his attention wanders; he can hear the old man's voice *like a stream* but is more concerned to stare at the being who seemed

Like one whom I had met with in a dream;
Or like a Man from some far region sent;
To give me human strength, and strong admonishment. (117–119)

Thus the old man takes on a symbolic significance. This transformation is central to the poem and can be compared to a similar situation presented in the poem *Michael* where, through the central character – an old shepherd – we view the hardships of rural life, of old age, of thwarted plans, and of desertion by children. The predicament of that shepherd symbolizes the experience of others. Wordsworth's belief in the social value of *Michael* and other poems which are concerned with the breakdown of the family unit is illustrated by the fact that in January 1801 he wrote to James Fox (the leader of the Whig – later known as Liberal – political party) asking him to read *Michael*; his accompanying letter makes it clear that by such action he was hoping to make the decision makers aware of the predicament of the poor. But, in spite of gaining such significance, Michael can be interpreted within the poem as an actual character struggling against circumstances. And the same is true of the leech gatherer who is presented as both a symbol and a credible, if somewhat strange, individual.

In stanza 18 of *Resolution and Independence* Wordsworth repeats his question to the leech gatherer, and this time hears the response. But we are not told what the old man says because that is not the important part of the poem. It is not what the old man says that is important but rather what he is. When the old man is finished the poet comments:

> I could have laughed myself to scorn, to find
> In that decrepit Man so firm a mind.
> 'God,' said I, 'be my help and stay secure;
> I'll think of the Leech-gatherer on the lonely moor.'   (144–147)

These lines drive home the truth of the experience for the poet. The leech gatherer is able to keep his dignity despite his circumstances and surroundings; the qualities that Wordsworth admires in the old man are stated in the title of the poem.

However, it is not the abstract moral concerns which stay with us after reading this poem, but rather the presentation of the leech gatherer and the landscape in which he appears. This point is emphasized by Wordsworth in a letter defending the poem to Sarah Hutchinson, his wife's sister:

> It is in the character of the old man to tell his story in a manner which an impatient reader must necessarily feel as tedious. But, Good God! Such a figure in such a place, a pious self-respecting, miserably infirm, and [*word illegible in MS*] Old Man telling such a tale!   (14 June 1802)

Just as the leech gatherer in *Resolution and Independence* leaves a vivid impression on the poet's imagination, so in *The Solitary Reaper* the poet acknowledges that he carries with him in his heart the song of the isolated unknown singer *Long after it was heard no more*.

The isolation of the figure in *The Solitary Reaper* is stressed in the title as well as the opening stanza of the poem by words like *single* and *alone*. But on this occasion it is not the appearance of the figure that arrests the poet – no external, personal features come through – but rather the haunting quality of her song. Here the poet does not question the figure. He does not understand the language she is singing and therefore is conscious of the words only as sound patterns which reinforce the melodic line of the song. He is content to listen and then to pass on.

In both *The Solitary Reaper* and *Resolution and Independence* the figures seem to be part of the landscape, part of nature itself. But in reading these pieces we cannot forget that the poet himself is also present as a participant in the action and not merely as an observer. In the latter Wordsworth questions the old man, and in the former he exhorts us to join him in viewing the scene and hearing the beautiful song.

Wordsworth is offering us in these poems a very individual presentation of the relationship between people and nature, which on occasions takes on the spiritual quality of a vision characterized by a strong sense of unity. Some readers find it difficult to relate to this spiritual aspect of Wordsworth's response, while others view it as a strength of his writings. You will have to consider carefully your own reactions to this issue in order to come to your own conclusions about Wordsworth as a nature poet.

Wordsworth and Childhood

Wordsworth's enthusiasm for nature was linked to his preoccupation with the insights and experiences of childhood. Children were seen to perceive the world in a way that was clear of adult distortions – an idea related to the theories of Jean-Jacques Rousseau who had a powerful influence on opinion in the second half of the eighteenth century. Rousseau believed that man was by nature good, a condition undermined by the influence of society, which was seen to be responsible for separating men from nature by making them disguise their true feelings. It followed from such theories that children, by virtue of their closeness to nature, might 'know' more than adults who had grown away from nature's influence. Wordsworth was concerned to explore the relationship between the experience of a child and the experience of an adult, as well as the mental growth that enables one state to emerge out of the other. His own poetic autobiography *The Prelude* was aptly subtitled by his wife *Growth of a Poet's Mind*.

'Anecdote for Fathers' and 'We Are Seven'

On occasions a young child and old man appear side by side in Wordsworth's poems, and the result serves to emphasize the differences rather than the similarities between the two. We will begin here by looking at two poems in which an adult questions a child: *Anecdote for Fathers* and *We Are Seven*.

In *Anecdote for Fathers* the poet is walking with a five-year-old boy. He asks the boy whether he would rather be where they are at present, at Liswyn Farm, or at Kilve by the sea, a place visited by both previously. The boy answers that he would rather be at Kilve and then he is pressed by Wordsworth for the reasons for his choice. The child is quite naturally unable to defend his response, but finally in desperation points to the fact that Kilve has no weather-cock – obviously the first thing that came into his head – as his reason for choosing that place. Lying is the natural resort of a child who is pushed too far – a lesson that is outlined in the sub-title. In the final stanza the poet presents himself as a curious observer, ready to learn from the child.

This same curiosity is found in *We Are Seven* in which an adult is presented with a child's view of death which clashes with his own. The opening stanza states the subject of the poem:

> A simple child, dear brother Jim,
> That lightly draws its breath,
> And feels its life in every limb,
> What should it know of death?   (1–4)

The little girl in this poem is not interested in the idea of death. In reply to the poet's questions about how many brothers and sisters she has, she replies she is one of seven children. In the course of conversation it becomes clear that two of her brothers and sisters are buried in the churchyard, but although the poet attempts to make the little girl view herself as one of five not seven, she sticks ardently to seven. Within this poem, Wordsworth is not claiming that all children think about death in this way; he is, rather, relating one particular incident.

Some critics have argued that the trivial nature of such an incident makes it unsuitable material for poetry, and have dismissed these two poems – and others which are also characterized by plain unsophisticated language and simplicity of content – as insignificant nonsense. But Wordsworth was confident of his judgement in including these compositions in a collection of poems entitled *Lyrical Ballads*. (See pp. 156–9 for details of this publication.) Before the volume went to press he was urged by a friend not to include *We Are Seven* on the grounds that it could make him look ridiculous – but Wordsworth was still ready to let the poem *take its chance*.

A defence of *We Are Seven* and similar poems was presented by William Hazlitt in an essay which appeared in 1825 in which he stated *the incidents are trifling . . . the reflections are profound*. Both *We Are Seven* and *Anecdote for Fathers* bring attention to the simplicity of the child's view and the way in which it differs from the view held by the adult. The implication is that children, being nearer to nature, might intuitively 'know' more than adults who have been in the world longer. In both instances the poet reveals that through listening to the child's responses he has gained an insight into a view of life that is different from his own.

The Lucy Poems

One particular child is at the centre of an intriguing group of five poems known as the Lucy poems. Critics have spent much time discussing whether Lucy was an actual person and, if so, what was her relationship with Wordsworth – but this debate has not, as yet, provided a satisfactory explanation. (See note on p. 107 for a brief discussion of Lucy's identity.) These poems are, however, important because they reveal a different perspective on Wordsworth's presentation of childhood in his poems.

Before turning our attention to this group of five poems, it will help to look first at a ballad entitled *Lucy Gray*. Here we are given an introduction to the figure who appears in the Lucy poems. *Lucy Gray* is memorable for its simplicity and for the unearthly quality of its subject. Our first glimpse of Lucy is as a *solitary* figure in a landscape. She is described as being at home in the open air, but by the end of the third stanza it becomes obvious that something awful has happened to her. As the ballad unfolds it is revealed that Lucy was lost on an errand. Despite the evidence which suggests that Lucy drowned, the poem closes on a supernatural note stating that some believe that the child's spirit can be seen roaming *Upon the lonesome Wild*. We can now turn to the five Lucy poems – 'A *slumber did my spirit seal*', *Song*, '*Strange fits of passion I have known*', '*Three years she grew in sun and shower*' and '*I travelled among unknown Men*'.

Activity

Read through the Lucy poems and make a note of any features that are common to the main female figure.

Discussion

Closeness to nature, isolation and death are concerns that reappear in these poems. Lucy's closeness to nature is suggested by the appearance of natural images – for example, in *'Three years she grew in sun and shower'* she is compared to a flower, in *Song* she is described as a half-hidden violet and in *'Strange fits of passion I have known'* she is compared to a rose – each of which serves to emphasize her beauty whilst implying that she, like the flower, will inevitably perish. In four of the group the girl dies, and in the fifth *'Strange fits of passion I have known'* her death is alluded to in the poet's cry *If Lucy should be dead*!

Each of this group is linked with the traditional ballad form – a poetic structure in which a story unfolds. Four of the Lucy poems are in quatrains with alternate lines rhyming; the exception *'Three years she grew in sun and shower'* extends the stanza to six lines by the introduction of couplets in lines 1 and 2 plus lines 4 and 5. The structural links with ballad form are, therefore, strong, but expectations of a straightforward narration are undermined on occasions by an element of ambiguity and a more meditative tone than one would expect from such a form. The opening line of *'Three years she grew in sun and shower'* offers an interesting example here.

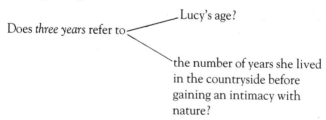

Does *three years* refer to

Lucy's age?

the number of years she lived in the countryside before gaining an intimacy with nature?

We are left wondering at the end if the poem is concerned with a dead girl becoming part of nature or with a living girl's closeness to nature. Such questions invite us to return to these poems again and again. The focus in the Lucy poems is very different from what is presented in *We Are Seven* and *Anecdote for Fathers*. There the poet is seen as a detached, curious observer; here Wordsworth includes complex emotional responses.

Intimations of Immortality

The above comments suggest that the Lucy poems are not as straightforward as they may appear at first glance. Another poem which offers complications to the reader, but which is neverthe-less important to consider within a discussion of Wordsworth's view of childhood, is the ode that begins *There was a time* – a composition which in 1815 was given the fuller title of *Ode: Intimations of Immortality from Recollections of Early Childhood*. Also in 1815 three lines from *My heart leaps up* were added as an epigraph to the poem:

> The Child is Father of the Man;
> And I could wish my days to be
> Bound each to each by natural piety. (7–9)

These lines emphasize a sense of continuity between childhood and adulthood. The child's view of the world is linked to what is experienced by the adult, and attention is drawn to the relationship between the two. Wordsworth calls for the bond to be one of *natural piety* – a reference to the bond of respect and love we naturally owe to our parents which Wordsworth feels he owes to his childhood.

This ode links the death of childhood with a corresponding loss of joy. The perspective of childhood through which aspects of nature seemed to be *Apparelled in celestial light* is now over for the poet, and as the poem progresses he makes clear his feelings of loss and regret. Childhood is here associated with a way of seeing which was brilliant and alive, a time of insight that Wordsworth refers to as *visionary gleam*, a phrase which combines the vivid and fleeting nature of the experience.

In the fifth stanza of the Intimations Ode, Wordsworth offers a philosophy of childhood which is based on his experience of life and the process of ageing. He suggests that the new-born child comes to this world from an earlier heavenly existence of which the child carries clear recollections. But as the child grows older the memories fade and eventually the child forgets – though it does at certain times have rare glimpses of its earlier glorious state. In his enthusiasm to emphasize the importance of the

child's position, Wordsworth addresses his subject in the
following terms:

> Thou, whose exterior semblance doth belie
> Thy Soul's immensity;
> Thou best Philosopher, who yet dost keep
> Thy heritage, thou Eye among the blind,
> That, deaf and silent, read'st the eternal deep,
> Haunted for ever by the eternal mind,—
> Mighty Prophet! Seer blest!
> On whom those truths do rest,
> Which we are toiling all our lives to find;   (108–116)

Such an address could be viewed, for example, as pretentious
rhetoric or as a successful attempt to emphasize the heights to
which Wordsworth elevated the state of childhood. The criteria
for such judgements need to be considered carefully.

In the Intimations Ode Wordsworth argues that the process of
ageing takes us further away from our initial exalted state. Ageing
is inevitably linked with decay, but Wordsworth does not end the
poem on a depressing note. In the final lines he dwells on the
pleasure that he has yet to enjoy during the few moments of
insight that are still within his grasp.

Here we are left in no doubt as to the importance that
Wordsworth attached to childhood. The poem contains a
mixture of simple, powerful statements on the subject:

> There was a time when meadow, grove, and stream,
> The earth, and every common sight,
> To me did seem
> Apparelled in celestial light,
> The glory and the freshness of a dream.   (1–5)

– as well as grandiose claims for its importance:

> The Youth, who daily farther from the East
> Must travel, still is Nature's Priest,
> And by the vision splendid
> Is on his way attended;   (71–74)

Childhood was a subject that Wordsworth returned to many times during his long career. When contrasted with the ordinariness of adult perception, the vividness associated with childhood took on a visionary quality for the poet.

Wordsworth in his Time

Wordsworth grew up in the Lake District in the eighteenth century, and although he spent periods of his life away from the area, it was in the Lake District that he died in 1850 at the age of 80 with a reputation that established him as one of the major poets of his time.

His lifetime spanned a period of political, social and religious upheaval. Events of these years – the French Revolution that shook the old order in France and reached its first climax with the storming of the Bastille in 1789, the Napoleonic Wars which were originally undertaken to defend and then spread the fruits of the French Revolution, and the Industrial Revolution – influenced the Romantic movement which transformed the arts in Europe in the late eighteenth and early nineteenth century.

This reference to a 'movement' might mistakenly be interpreted as a group of writers working with agreed objectives, but this was definitely not the case with Wordsworth and other leading writers of the period – Blake, Coleridge, Byron, Keats and Shelley – who emerged as poets of the Romantic Age in England; during their own lifetimes they were certainly not conscious of being members of a recognizable literary group. However, despite this proviso, it is possible to outline some of the general attitudes which these poets share and which can be seen as characteristic traits of the Romantic movement:

a concern for personal experience

an intensity of feeling

a belief in the central role of the imagination

The third point, concerning the role of the imagination, was a move away from the previously accepted view of the imagination as a faculty concerned with passively reflecting nature through art. To Wordsworth and his contemporaries the imagination was a powerful creative force capable of interacting with the external world in a way that enabled the poet to see beyond what was immediately obvious into the very essence of things.

Wordsworth's formal education included time at Hawkshead Grammar School (previously in Lancashire, now in Cumbria), and at Cambridge University. Education of a more informal kind came through travel and the influence of political and literary figures of his day.

Wordsworth's studies at St John's College, Cambridge, held little attraction for him. His vacations, however, especially when he travelled in France and Switzerland, were times that he looked back on with enthusiasm. Pressure was put on him by his guardians – his parents being dead – to enter a profession, but the Law, the Church and the Army were each rejected. When he had finished at Cambridge Wordsworth chose to spend some time travelling; he moved to London and then on to France, and in the year he spent there – 1791–1792 – the country, in the midst of revolution, saw the overthrow of the monarchy and the declaration of the Republic. Whilst in France, Wordsworth fell in love with Annette Vallon, a French girl who gave birth to his daughter. By Autumn 1792 Wordsworth's money had run out so he returned to England without Annette and his child, and in the following year England declared war on France.

Year	Wordsworth	Year	Historical events
1799	Rents Dove Cottage, Grasmere	1799	Napoleon becomes First Consul
1800	Second Edition of *Lyrical Ballads* in 2 volumes	1802	Temporary peace between England and France
1802	Marries Mary Hutchinson (4 Oct)	1804	Napoleon becomes Emperor
		1805	Battle of Trafalgar
1805	Wordsworth's brother John drowns		
1807	*Poems in Two Volumes* published		
1808	Moves to Allan Bank, Grasmere		
1810	Quarrels with Coleridge		
1811	Moves to the Rectory, Grasmere		
1812	Reconciled with Coleridge		
1813	Moves to Rydal Mount		
1815	Appointed Distributor of Stamps (tax collector) for Westmorland	1815	Waterloo. End of Napoleonic Wars
1819	First collected edition of *Poems* Appointed J. P.	1820	George IV takes the throne
1827	*Poetical Works* published	1830	William IV takes the throne
1834	Death of Coleridge	1837	Victoria takes the throne
1842	Civil list pension of £300 p.a.		
1843	Appointed Poet Laureate		
1850	Dies at Rydal Mount		

Chronology

The time-chart below offers a skeleton of events in Wordsworth's life listed against what was happening in British and European history, to help you put Wordsworth's life into an appropriate context and give you background to the changing focus of his writing.

Events in Wordsworth's Life

1770	Birth of William Wordsworth at Cockermouth, Cumbria (7 April)
1778	Mother dies
1779	Sent to Hawkshead Grammar School (until 1787)
1783	Father dies
1787	At St John's College, Cambridge (until 1791)
1790	Spends vacation touring France and Switzerland
1791	Leaves Cambridge with a Pass Degree. Returns to France
1792	Birth of illegitimate daughter to Annette Vallon
1795	Inherits £900 from Raisley Calver whom Wordsworth had nursed before his death
	First meeting with Coleridge
	Settles with his sister Dorothy in Dorset
1797	Moves to Alfoxden House, Somerset
1798	Walking tour in Wye Valley
	Visits Tintern Abbey
	Publication of *Lyrical Ballads*
	Visits Germany (stays until April 1799)

Other Events

1789	French Revolution begins
1791	Louis XVI imprisoned
1792	Birth of Shelley
1793	England at war with France
1795	Birth of Keats

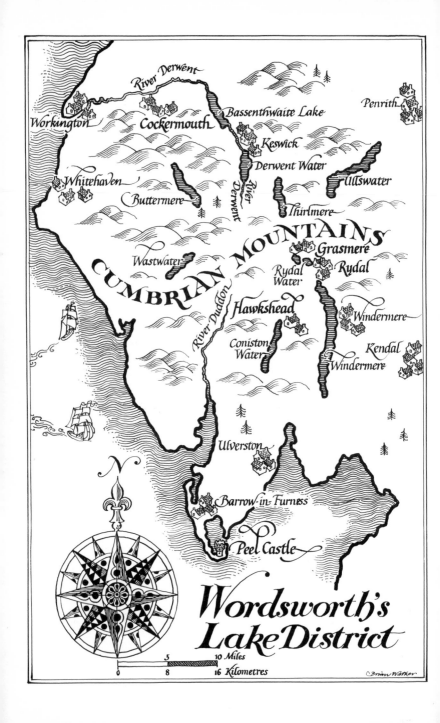

River Derwent

Workington

Cockermouth

Bassenthwaite Lake

Penrith

Keswick

Derwent Water

Whitehaven

River Derwent

Ullswater

Buttermere

Thirlmere

CUMBRIAN MOUNTAINS

Grasmere

Wastwater

Rydal Water

Rydal

River Duddon

Hawkshead

Windermere

Coniston Water

Kendal

Windermere

Ulverston

N

Barrow-in-Furness

Peel Castle

Wordsworth's Lake District

5   10 Miles

0   8   16 Kilometres

Brian Walker

Political belief

In the early 1790s Wordsworth was part of the Left wing of English politics, a passionate supporter of the French Revolution and of democracy. The British parliamentary system, then still unreformed, could hardly be described as democratic. The real power lay in the hands of aristocratic landowners like the Lowther family, or Earls of Lonsdale, who owned a substantial area of Cumberland. Wordsworth's father had worked for the Lowthers; he was officially described as a 'law-agent' but at the time of elections ensuring political support for his Tory employer was a major consideration.

In later years Wordsworth was seen to 'change sides' as he supported the Right of British politics with a fervour equal to that he had shown previously in support of the Left. In 1818 Wordsworth, now settled in the Lake District with his sister Dorothy, wife Mary and children, worked in the general election for the new Lord Lowther, who had repaid a debt owing to the family that had been outstanding since the death of Wordsworth's father, and in 1819 Wordsworth became Justice of the Peace for Westmorland. Such a move caused him to be viewed by some poets as a traitor to the cause of freedom, an attitude reflected in Robert Browning's poem *The Lost Leader* (1845), the last stanza of which opens with the words:

Just for a handful of silver he left us,
Just for a riband to stick in his coat . . .

This reference to *a handful of silver* echoes the details of Judas Iscariot's betrayal of Christ, and thus makes clear Browning's loathing of Wordsworth's move to the Right.

There has been much speculation concerning the reasons for Wordsworth's change of sides – some have suggested moral cowardice, others personal gain – but whatever his motivation, there is ample evidence in his poetry that Wordsworth was politically conscious throughout his life. '*I grieved for Buonaparte*' and *Thought of a Briton on the Subjugation of Switzerland* offer obvious examples: both reveal his growing disillusionment with Napoleon Buonaparte who was General-in-Chief of the French Army 1796–1799. As Napoleon's military reputation and power grew, he alienated Wordsworth and many others who had previously admired his achievements and his stand for liberty. Napoleon was seen as being responsible for diverting France away from a concern for liberty and revolution through pursuing an aggressive foreign policy. The dilemma was highlighted in 1798 when the Swiss, a nation who symbolized liberty for Wordsworth, were brought under the control of France – a move by liberty against liberty! In 1804 Napoleon declared himself Emperor, and many shared Wordsworth's disgust at this turn of events, including Beethoven, who tore out the dedication of his Eroica Symphony.

Wordsworth's family life

As well as finding poems within this selection which reflect Wordsworth's awareness of contemporary political events, you will also discover compositions that reflect on stages of the poet's own life and that of his immediate family. *Nutting*, for example, was written during Wordsworth's stay in Germany in 1798: it was intended as part of his autobiographical poem *The Prelude*, but was later omitted. In the poem he thinks back to the time when he attended Hawkshead Grammar School. He remembers a day on which he went off alone in search of nuts. The violence of his efforts to gain nuts is contrasted to the quiet beauty of the nut tree before he begins his assault, and the young Wordsworth is left with a *sense of pain* suggesting that he has learnt from the experience and has gained a sense of respect for what nature has to offer.

Another example is found in *Elegiac Stanzas* in which Wordsworth describes how his view of life has changed as the result of the loss of his brother John, drowned in 1805 when the ship he captained sank in a storm off the Dorset coast. The poet remembers the impact of that event in the line *A deep distress hath humanized my Soul* (36); within the poem he compares his earlier attitude to life with the approach that he has now adopted under the shadow of his feeling of loss. The poem ends, however, on an optimistic note as Wordsworth welcomes *fortitude* and *patience*, and accepts his new approach to life with resignation.

Literary friends

Wordsworth had a wide circle of literary friends. His house, as indicated by numerous references in his sister's journal, was often overflowing with guests and he also made trips away from the Lake District to visit contemporary writers. A number of the meetings were recorded and the results make interesting reading for those curious to discover the kind of figure Wordsworth presented to his visitors. The following was written by William Hazlitt who first met Wordsworth in 1798:

> He was quaintly dressed (according to the costume of that unconstrained period) in a brown fustian jacket and striped pantaloons . . . There was a severe, worn pressure of thought about his temples, a fire in his eye (as if he saw something in objects more than outward appearance), an intense, high, narrow forehead, a Roman nose, cheeks furrowed by a strong purpose, and a convulsive inclination to laughter about the mouth, a good deal at variance with the solemn, stately expression of the rest of his face . . .

That same account also comments on Wordsworth's accent, his *northern burr*. Within Wordsworth's poems dialect expressions are not a cause of real difficulty, but occasional rhymes (*notes* and *thoughts* for instance) serve to remind the reader of the poet's northern links.

Samuel Taylor Coleridge was one of Wordsworth's closest friends. The two poets first met in Bristol in 1795; by that time Coleridge had already left Jesus College Cambridge (without a degree) and was closely involved in literary and political activity. In 1797 Wordsworth and Dorothy rented Alfoxden, a large house in Somerset, to be near Coleridge and his family. Wordsworth and Coleridge were clearly 'radicals' in their thinking and appearance, and the suspicion the two aroused at that time is illustrated by the fact that a government spy was sent to report on their activities following rumours that the two were supporters of an extreme French revolutionary society!

The friendship spanned a time of great poetic activity for both writers. They worked together on a collection of poems entitled *Lyrical Ballads* which appeared in its first edition in 1798. (See pp. 156–9 for discussion of this publication.) Coleridge's contribution included *The Ancient Mariner* which was given prominence by being placed at the front of that first edition. The stages of collaboration in this venture are outlined at length by Coleridge in his *Biographia Literaria* (1817), a publication that includes an element of philosophical enquiry plus details of Coleridge's own life, the history of his literary opinions and comments on Wordsworth's writings. (An extract from *Biographia Literaria* appears on p. 104 in a note on *The Idiot Boy*.) The relationship ended with a quarrel in 1810, and although there was a later reconciliation the friendship never re-established its original fervour. In 1835, a year after Coleridge's death, Wordsworth wrote *Extempore Effusion Upon the Death of James Hogg*, a touching poem which points to the strength of the poets' friendship and makes reference to many other literary figures of the day. (See p. 124 for further details.)

Dorothy and her journals

One person who remained devoted to Wordsworth throughout was his sister Dorothy. She had been brought up in the care of various relatives before setting up house with Wordsworth in 1794. As well as travelling with her brother, she also organized the many daily chores of the Wordsworth household, and continued to live in the family house after Wordsworth's marriage to Mary Hutchinson. For many years Dorothy kept journals giving details of day-to-day life and making references to the creation of Wordsworth's poems. The following extracts are from entries for 1802, taken from Mary Moorman's edition of the journals (Oxford University Press, 1971):

> I was starching small linen all the morning. It snowed a good deal and was terribly cold. After dinner it was fair, but I was obliged to run all the way to the foot of the White Moss to get the least bit of warmth into me . . . I got tea when I reached home and then set on to reading German. I wrote part of a letter to Coleridge, went late to bed and slept badly.   (15 February 1802)

> A divine morning. At Breakfast Wm wrote part of an ode. Mr Olliff sent the dung and Wm went to work in the garden. We sate all day in the orchard.   (27 March 1802)

> A very warm gentle morning . . . a little rain. Wm wrote two sonnets on Buonaparte after I had read Milton's sonnets to him. In the evening . . . I planted about the well − was much heated and I think I caught cold.   (21 May 1802)

The journals are well worth looking at in more detail. They offer an insight into life in the Wordsworth household as well as glimpses of the literary figures of the day who visited the family.

A careful reading of these journals makes it clear that frequently ideas from Wordsworth's poems came from this source. (An extract from Dorothy's journal relating to the composition of '*I wandered lonely as a Cloud*' is given on p. 135.) Dorothy wrote poems herself but was not satisfied with them; however, the journals remain a memorial to her close and strikingly vivid observation of nature. Unfortunately, Dorothy's mental health deteriorated in the 1830s; she never fully recovered, but nevertheless outlived her brother and died in 1855.

During his long life, Wordsworth wrote travel guides, essays and letters on a wide variety of subjects, but within the literary world his mark was made most forcibly by his comments about his own poems − and it is these comments which provide the focus for the following section.

Wordsworth's Language

A determination to use language in a way that was different from his contemporaries established Wordsworth as a pioneer early in his poetic career.

The kind of writing that Wordsworth was reacting against is illustrated by the opening lines of Thomas Gray's *Sonnet on the Death of Richard West* which was first published in 1742:

> In vain to me the smiling mornings shine,
> And reddening Phoebus lifts his golden fire:
> The birds in vain their amorous descant join,
> Or cheerful fields resume their green attire.

Wordsworth saw nothing to praise in the elaborate language of these lines. He attacked what he labelled as *gaudiness and inane phraseology* and made a plea for simplicity, a quality that is clearly lacking from a line like *And reddening Phoebus lifts his golden fire*.

Lyrical Ballads

His original and revolutionary approach was made apparent in *Lyrical Ballads*, a volume of poems which was published anonymously in 1798 as a result of a collaboration with Coleridge. In these poems Wordsworth was making a conscious effort to avoid the extravagant and artificial language – the *poetic diction* that he commented on at length in his 1802 Appendix to the Preface to *Lyrical Ballads* – of much conventional eighteenth-century poetry. Wordsworth was aiming at making poetic vocabulary less remote from ordinary speech.

The title of *Lyrical Ballads* refers to ballads (simple narrative poems) and lyrics (short poems of personal feelings) – but it is not possible to divide the contents neatly under these two headings. Qualities of both these forms are combined in the poems so that most show characteristics of one form more strongly than the other. A reading of *The Idiot Boy*, for example, reveals the strong narrative framework of the ballad form; the story unfolds in simple stanzas of the kind that appears opposite:

The silence of her idiot boy,
What hopes it sends to Betty's heart!
He's at the guide-post − he turns right,
She watches till he's out of sight,
And Betty will not then depart.   (102–106)

In these lines there are no words that are difficult to understand; here we see the everyday language that is a characteristic of many − but not all − of the poems that appeared in the 1798 volume, plus the poet's interest in people − not the aristocrats or great literary figures of the time, but rather ordinary people as well as the outcasts and the rejected.

The Idiot Boy was the subject of much discussion at the time of its initial publication. The language used by Wordsworth to express the sounds made by the boy − *burr, burr* − was offensive to some readers who wanted more emphasis on the boy's beauty rather than attempts to capture his idiocy. (See p. 104 for a fuller discussion of such objections to *The Idiot Boy* and Wordsworth's reactions to them.)

The lyrical element of *Lyrical Ballads* comes to the fore in the second edition of the volume which appeared in 1800. This edition is divided into two volumes, the second containing many new poems which stress an emotional response with little emphasis on story. A consideration of the language used in the opening line of *Song* ('*She dwelt among th'untrodden ways*'), one of the Lucy poems, reveals some of the tensions that are a characteristic of these short compositions. Why *dwelt* instead of *lived*? How can *ways* be *untrodden*? You may remember similar points emerging from the discussion of '*Three years she grew in sun and shower*' on p. 143. For some readers such oddities create problems that take the attention too far from the text; for others these ambiguities of language are an essential part of the fascination of the Lucy poems.

To these ballads and lyrics should, of course, be added the poems in blank verse (lines of ten syllables without rhyme) which are represented in *Lyrical Ballads* most notably by *Michael* and *Tintern Abbey*. A close look at the language used in the opening section of *Tintern Abbey* (lines 1–23) reveals that here Wordsworth is concerned to present the reader with the specific detail of a particular landscape. As the description unfolds we hear the poet sharpening the details using language that seems more typical of Thomas Gray than of the author of *The Idiot Boy* and the Lucy poems:

> Once again I see
> These hedge-rows, hardly hedge-rows, little lines
> Of sportive wood run wild;   (15–17)

In these lines the notion of neat hedgerows is rejected in favour of a fanciful image which attempts to capture the unpredictable curling lines of trees which divide one field from another.

Ballads, lyrical compositions and the use of blank verse for contemplative poetry were all familiar to the reading public at the end of the eighteenth century, but the poems which appeared in *Lyrical Ballads* were, nevertheless, a conscious attempt to write in a new way. The emphasis in a number of the poems seemed to be on writing in a deliberately unpoetical language, an affront to the eighteenth-century sense of decorum. Compare the lines from Thomas Gray's *Sonnet on the Death of Richard West* which appear on p. 156 with any lines from *We Are Seven, Anecdote for Fathers* or *The Idiot Boy*, for example, and the difference is made clear. Indeed, Wordsworth went as far as to state that in his opinion – one that many have argued against since – there is no real difference between the language of poetry and the language of prose.

Advertisement (1798) *and* Preface (1800 and 1802)

In the 1798 publication of *Lyrical Ballads*, Wordsworth included an Advertisement which outlined some of the principles upon which the poems were composed. This comparatively short introduction was greatly expanded into a Preface for the 1800 edition, and yet more additions were made for a later 1802 edition. Before discussing some of the more important points made in the later editions, I think it would be helpful to summarize the ideas contained in the 1798 Advertisement:

> 1. If a subject interests the human mind, it is possible material for poetry.

> 2. The poems in the collection are 'experiments' using language such as would be found in the conversations of real people.

> 3. The reader is asked not to dismiss the poems because of their unusual nature, but rather to read them carefully, if possible with an open mind.

The later expanded Preface makes demanding but fascinating reading. It touches on the points outlined above but adds much more: Wordsworth raises many questions and deals with each with confidence and energy. For example, he defends his decision to use language and situations from *low and rustic* life, and states that the language of poetry should be *a selection of the language really spoken by men*. The word *selection* is important here: the language in Wordsworth's poems draws upon everyday speech which, although it may appear to capture the naturalness of conversation, is the result of careful selection and the powers of the imagination. Wordsworth also attempts to define what makes a poet, and on this last point he has some particularly interesting things to say.

In answer to the question *What is a poet?* he writes *He is a man speaking to men*. The argument is later elaborated: . . . *the Poet is chiefly distinguished from other men by a greater promptness to think and feel without immediate external excitement, and a greater power in expressing such thoughts and feelings as are produced in him in that manner*. The phrase *without immediate external excitement* refers to the creative process in which the poet is not reacting directly to an external stimulus, but is rather recollecting that experience at a later date when he is writing poetry, a process outlined in '*I wandered lonely as a Cloud*', for example.

159

In the same Preface Wordsworth defines poetry as *the spontaneous overflow of powerful feelings*. By this he does not mean that poetry should be the uncontrolled outpouring of emotion. He argues that a period of contemplation is necessary to the creation of the finest poetry. The creative process that he is outlining begins with *emotion recollected in tranquillity*; under such conditions the poet has the power to recreate the original emotion to a point where he seems almost to be reliving the experience, and thus he achieves a mood in which the creative activity can take place. The original emotion has now been affected by thought and thus, between the actual experience and the poetic activity, there has been a time for modification and selection of material which has included the involvement of the memory and the imagination. By this stage in the argument, it has become obvious that despite his earlier protestations Wordsworth is making the poet into a man apart. He is putting aside the established critical view of that time (based on an ancient Greek assumption) that art is an activity concerned with imitating or mirroring nature, and is suggesting that poetry may be achieved not so much from imitating nature but rather from imaginatively recreating it. In Wordsworth's view the poet possesses special imaginative powers and great sensitivity, and thus although he is a *man speaking to men* he is definitely a man apart from others.

This changed perception of what a poem is and does, and of the role of the poet, has been commented on influentially by M. H. Abrams in a book entitled *The Mirror and the Lamp: Romantic Theory and the Critical Tradition* (1953). Abrams argues that the changed perception is what distinguishes a Romantic writer from an eighteenth-century writer, and he presents Wordsworth as a figure who heralds details of the changes in his Preface to the *Lyrical Ballads* of 1800.

The poems grouped between *Lines, Written at a Small Distance from my House* and *Michael* in this chronological selection of Wordsworth's poems are some of the pieces which were originally published in *Lyrical Ballads*. As you re-read these poems think carefully about the ideas that Wordsworth was proposing at the time of their composition about the kind of language and subjects appropriate to poetry.

Activity

Read *Goody Blake and Harry Gill* and *Tintern Abbey*. Taking these as your example, do you think that Wordsworth achieves the simplicity he was aiming at in all of his poems in *Lyrical Ballads*?

Discussion

The opening of *Goody Blake and Harry Gill* establishes clearly Wordsworth's use of simple, conversational language typical of ballad form:

> Oh! what's the matter? what's the matter?
> What is't that ails young Harry Gill?
> That evermore his teeth they chatter,
> Chatter, chatter, chatter still. (1–4)

The rhymes are obvious, and the rhyme of *Gill* and *still* is one that reappears more than once as the poem progresses. There are echoes in these lines of the strong narrative framework of the ballad form that has already been noted in *The Idiot Boy*. (See pp. 156–7 above.)

The directness and simplicity of *Goody Blake and Harry Gill* contrast sharply with the following lines from *Tintern Abbey*:

> And I have felt
> A presence that disturbs me with the joy
> Of elevated thoughts; a sense sublime
> Of something far more deeply interfused . . (94–97)

This is obviously not language from *low and rustic* life. Such lines from *Tintern Abbey* make it clear that Wordsworth did not follow his theory of language on every occasion; he was ready to use language as complex as the subject required.

The above discussion suggests that Wordsworth was not consistent in applying the principles outlined in the Preface to all his poems in *Lyrical Ballads*. The direct language of *Goody Blake and Harry Gill* reinforced by repetition within the framework of a ballad contrasts clearly with the lines of blank verse from *Tintern Abbey* which contain abstract reflective language – what Coleridge referred to as Wordsworth's *impassioned, lofty and sustained diction*. A popular response to this is to wonder at the fact that Wordsworth chose to publish such different pieces in a single volume, and to argue that Wordsworth's poetry is at its best when in *Tintern Abbey* for example he forgets, or perhaps one should say surmounts, his theories.

Reaction from contemporaries

Wordsworth's tone in the Preface is outspoken and confident, and the work generated much discussion in contemporary literary circles. Southey's review which appeared in *The Critical Review* in October 1798 illustrates the kind of mixed response that the volume provoked. On *The Idiot Boy* he writes *No tale less deserves the labour that appears to have been bestowed upon this*, but he is ready to acknowledge *superior powers* in *Tintern Abbey*. The review ends:

> The 'experiment', we think, has failed, not because the language of conversation is little adapted to 'the purposes of poetic pleasure,' but because it has been tried upon uninteresting subjects. Yet every piece discovers genius; and, ill as the author has frequently employed his talents, they certainly rank him with the best of living poets.

Despite Southey's reservations about Wordsworth's choice of subjects, this final paragraph that appears above is by no means discouraging; but Wordsworth was displeased that Southey, his friend, should be less then wholeheartedly supportive of the venture. Wordsworth's letters suggest that he regarded public recognition as his due.

Wordsworth was very concerned that his poetry should be read carefully. Indeed, he had something to say on this point in a letter written in 1808 to Sir George Beaumont, a landscape painter. There he complains about the fact that a friend of the Beaumonts had described '*I wandered lonely as a Cloud*' as being *on daffodils reflected in the water*:

> My Language is precise . . . let me ask your Friend how it is possible for flowers to be reflected in water when there are waves? They may indeed in still water; but the very object of my poem is the trouble or agitation, both of the flowers and Water . . . my Poems must be more nearly looked at before they can give rise to any remarks of much value, even from the strongest minds.

Such a statement illustrates the importance he attached to the accuracy of language in his poems, and his conviction that his greatness would only be recognized by the astute and careful reader.

Later poems

Wordsworth was 28 when *Lyrical Ballads* first appeared, and there were therefore many years of poetry writing in front of him before his death at the age of 80. During his later years his output was vast, including many poems that reflect a change of approach and focus. Old age brought with it much concentration on the weakening imagination and the effect of personal tragedies, as seen in *Elegiac Stanzas* and *Extempore Effusion Upon the Death of James Hogg* for example; in these poems Wordsworth has moved away from the concern with simplicity and directness of language that characterized much of his earlier work. The achievement of these later poems is of a different kind from what is admired in *Lyrical Ballads*. There is evidence of more metrical variety in the poems as glimpsed in his elaborate ode forms and his sonnets. A strong moralizing voice echoes through poems like *The River Duddon: Conclusion* and *Mutability* which have been praised for their craftsmanship, but a lessening of intensity has also been noted.

Activity

Look for the qualities mentioned on p. 163 in the opening lines of *Mutability*:

> From low to high doth dissolution climb,
> And sinks from high to low, along a scale
> Of awful notes, whose concord shall not fail;
> A musical but melancholy chime,
> Which they can hear who meddle not with crime,
> Nor avarice, nor over-anxious care.   (1–6)

Discussion

The moralizing voice is clear here, as is the craftsmanship of these lines which develop into a carefully-constructed sonnet. Do you think these lines show a lessening of intensity? To what extent is your response to this question determined by your reaction to the idea explored within the lines?

Some critical responses

Wordsworth's poems have been the subject of much critical scrutiny concerning the stage at which his poetry was at its finest. The Victorians looked to Wordsworth for inspiration and comfort, and found that in the poet's appreciation of nature, particularly as found in his later poems – a point that is illustrated in the selection made by F. T. Palgrave for *The Golden Treasury* which was first published in 1861. More recent opinion has tended to argue that Wordsworth's early poems are finer than the late. Indeed, some have gone as far as to maintain that he wrote hardly anything worthwhile after 1805.

What reservations, if any, about Wordsworth's poems have you developed as a result of reading this selection? In your judgement, is there evidence in this chronological sequence of a point when the poems change markedly, either for the better or for the worse? A record of your own comments, made while rereading this selection, on the ideas and the way that Wordsworth presents and expresses them in his poems may help you to formulate your responses to the above questions.

Over the years Wordsworth's poems have been approached from many different perspectives. Francis Jeffrey, who edited the *Edinburgh Review* from 1803 to 1829, was one of Wordsworth's most outspoken critics. He viewed Wordsworth's ideas about the kind of language that was suitable for poetry as an attempt by Wordsworth to undermine the values of his time and the responsibilities of his class. Others in more recent years have seen much to praise in the way Wordsworth used language to celebrate the ordinary pleasures of rural people and rural living.

The poems have on different occasions been censured for their lack of sexuality, their narrowness of range and their lack of humour. Wordsworth himself has been criticized by some for being too much of a Christian poet and others have found fault with him for not being an orthodox enough Christian. It has also been argued that when Wordsworth defined the poet as *a man speaking to men* he was effectively, if unthinkingly, excluding women from poetic speech.

Different readers stress different things. It is worth asking yourself if such approaches add to your reading of Wordsworth's poems. Are these critics blaming Wordsworth for what he does not say rather than listening and responding to the poems themselves? This was certainly the view of Helen Darbishire, a recent Wordsworth scholar whose discussion of these poems (following Matthew Arnold's influential essay written in 1879) emphasized Wordsworth as a simple poet concerned with feelings and an essential humanity. Some critics, however, have held Arnold's view as telling only half the story and have followed the lead established by A. C. Bradley in his 1909 study of the complexities of Wordsworth's poems, the visionary aspects which lie beneath the surface of the writing.

M. H. Abrams, in his introduction to *Wordsworth: a Collection of Critical Essays* (1972), comments on two voices that can be heard in Wordsworth's own critical writing as well as in his poetry. Abrams sees evidence of these two distinct critical voices in Wordsworth's Preface to *Lyrical Ballads* and his *Essay, Supplementary to the Preface*, related to his *Poems* of 1815: in the first Wordsworth stresses a concern for the simple and universal; in the second he defends his poetic innovations by outlining what he sees as an *affinity between religion and poetry*, and by stressing the complex contradictions that are to be found in his poems.

Simplicity and complexity lie side by side in Wordsworth's poetry. Some readers have viewed such a combination as a strength, arguing that one aspect complements the other, whereas others have pointed to it as a fundamental weakness. You must decide on your own reaction to this and other issues that present themselves as you read and consider the material contained in this selection of Wordsworth's poems.

Further Reading

Gill, S., (ed.), *William Wordsworth* (Oxford: Oxford University Press (The Oxford Authors), 1984). A useful one-volume edition containing Wordsworth's poems arranged chronologically with helpful notes. The 1805 13-book version of The Prelude appears here outside the chronological sequence together with extracts from Wordsworth's prose.

Hayden, John O., (ed.), *William Wordsworth: Selected Prose* (Harmondsworth: Penguin, 1988). This offers most of what Wordsworth wrote in prose supported by helpful notes.

Moorman, Mary, (ed.), *Journals of Dorothy Wordsworth* (Oxford: Oxford University Press, 1971). Dorothy's Journals 1798–1803, plus an appendix of shorter poems by Wordsworth referred to in the journals and two poems by Dorothy herself.

*   *   *

Purkis, John, *A Preface to Wordsworth* (London: Longman, 1970 (rev. ed. 1986)). A useful general introduction to Wordsworth's life and work.

Gill, S., (ed.), *William Wordsworth: A Life* (Oxford: Clarendon Press, 1989). A detailed account of Wordsworth's life as a writer.

Butler, Marilyn, *Romantics, Rebels and Reactionairies* (Oxford: Oxford University Press, 1981). An informative discussion of English literature and its background 1760–1830.

Abrams, M. H., (ed.)., *Wordsworth: a Collection of Critical Essays* (New Jersey: Spectrum (Twentieth Century Views). 1972). A selection of critical essays on Wordsworth's poetry.

Barrell, John, 'The uses of Dorothy: "The Language of the Sense" in *Tintern Abbey* pp. 137–167 in *Poetry, Language and Politics*, (Manchester: Manchester University Press, 1988.) An essay about the language of *Tintern Abbey* – the language of natural description, and the language of contemplation – and about the way in which knowledge of assumptions about gender-difference can influence a reading of the poem.

Tasks

1 Read *Michael* and *Resolution and Independence* and then give your opinion of Wordsworth's strengths as a narrative poet.

2 Read the section in Approaches (pp. 130–39) which explores some of the ways in which nature is presented in Wordsworth's poems and consider the following poems in the light of that discussion: '*A whirl-blast from behind the hill*', *Expostulation and Reply*, *The Tables Turned* and *Lines, Composed at Grasmere*.

3 Wordsworth said of his poems that *the feeling therein developed gives importance to the action and situation, and not the action and situation to the feeling*. What is your reaction to this statement in the light of your reading of the poems in this selection?

4 Some critics have argued that the five Lucy poems – read the section in Approaches (pp. 142–3) for details – represent Wordsworth's greatest achievement; others have described these same poems as minor fragments without a context. Consider both these views and make clear your own reactions to the Lucy poems.

5 Do you agree that Wordsworth is easier to appreciate when he stops trying to be simple?

6 In this selection you will find thirteen of Wordsworth's sonnets. Read each of them and then, through a close discussion of two, consider Wordsworth's skill as a writer of sonnets.

7 Explain and illustrate the special importance that childhood held for Wordsworth.

8　Choose two or three poems from this collection that have made a particular impression on you. Give your opinion on the ideas and the way they are expressed and presented within each chosen poem.

9　To what extent do you agree that Wordsworth's main concern is the mystery of everyday life?

10　'Inseparable from Wordsworth's love of Nature is his love of people.' Discuss.

11　Gentleness. Austerity. Are these the qualities you have found in Wordsworth's poetry?

12　'Subject-matter determines style.' Consider two or three of Wordsworth's poems in the light of this statement.

13　There are two Voices: one is of the deep;
　　It learns the storm-cloud's thundrous melody,
　　Now roars, now murmurs with the changing sea,
　　Now bird-like pipes, now closes soft in sleep.
　　And one is of an old half-witted sheep
　　Which bleats articulate monotony,
　　And indicates that two and one are three,
　　That grass is green, lakes damp, and mountains steep.
　　And, Wordsworth, both are thine . . .

These lines, from *A Sonnet* by J. K. Stephen first published in 1891, parody Wordsworth's writings and introduce the notion of there being *two Voices* in Wordsworth's poetry – the poetically sublime and the poetically ridiculous. (You may find a reading of the opening chapter of F. W. Bateson's *Wordsworth: A Reinterpretation*, Longman, 1954 useful in exploring this idea in more detail.) Are there any poems in this selection that seem to you to be obvious contenders for either or both of these categories? Or do you think that such a notion is unhelpful to a consideration of Wordsworth's poetry? Argue your case carefully through close discussion of your chosen poems.

Max Beerbohm's cartoon entitled 'Wordsworth in the Lake District, at Cross Purposes'. (See page 105)

A drawing of William Wordsworth aged 35 by Thomas Edridge, 1805. (See page 151–2)

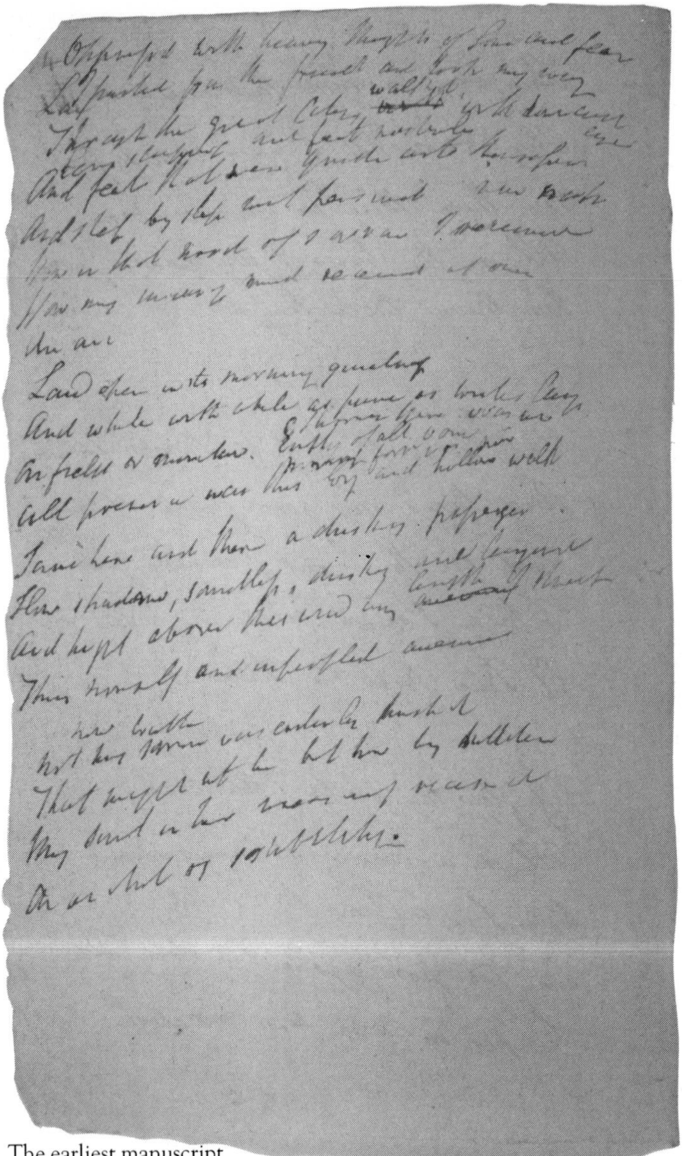

The earliest manuscript drafting of *St Pauls*. (See page 122)

Tintern Abbey, engraved by J. Smith from a drawing by G. Holmes, 1807. (See page 132)

'Peele Castle in a Storm' by George Beaumont – the painting referred to in Wordsworth's *Elegiac Stanzas*. (See page 120)

Index of Titles and First Lines